AF522081

ADMINISTRATION OF FOOD FOR WORK PROGRAMME

ADMINISTRATION OF FOOD FOR WORK PROGRAMME

By

Dr. Gundluru Thulasiram

M.A., Ph.D., PGDCA

Dept. of Political Science & Public Administration

Sri Venkateswara University

Tirupati - 517 502

(Andhra Pradesh)

(India)

DISCOVERY PUBLISHING HOUSE PVT. LTD.

NEW DELHI-110 002

Published by:
Tilak Wasan
DISCOVERY PUBLISHING HOUSE PVT. LTD.
4383/4B, Ansari Road, Darya Ganj
New Delhi-110 002 (India)
Phone : +91-11-23279245, 43596064-65
Fax : +91-11-23253475
E-mail : parul.wasan@gmail.com
discoverypublishinghouse@gmail.com
web : www.discoverypublishinggroup.com

***First Edition:* 2012**

ISBN: 978-93-5056-064-8

Administration of Food for Work Programme

Printed at:
Shree Balaji Art Press
Delhi

Dedicated To My Beloved
Parents
Smt. G. Manikyamma
&
Sri G. Iragaiah

Preface

The present study examines the extent to which the objective of the FFWP has been achieved with particular reference to the following. The extent of additional gainful employment generated in the rural areas. The changes income level of the beneficiaries. The contribution of the programme in creating durable community assets and providing infrastructure for rural development. The impact on farm prices and agricultural wages and Impact of the programme on the consumption level and nutritional intake of beneficiaries.

The usefulness of the programme is bringing about the social change in the village community in terms of meeting social obligations, social mobility. It will be seen that while keeping the main objectives of the programme in view, an attempt has been made in the evaluation study to widen the scope of the investigation by including some more items which have relevance larger national objectives.

The book is presented in six chapters. The first chapter deals with introduction to the research study.

The second chapter focuses on the beneficiaries of these programmes, District profile and selected mandals, distribution of food grains under Food for Work Programme.

The Third chapter is about Distribution of wages under the Food for Work Programme.

Operationalisation and Problems of Food for Work Programme is dealt in the Fourth chapter.

The Fifth chapter discusses the Monitoring and Evaluation of the Food for Work Programme.

Chapter Six gives the Summary and Conclusion.

The selected area for the study falls in Chittoor District of Andhra Pradesh. Both primary and secondary data were collected. To study the impact of the FFWP and an empirical study is carried out in the district. Two mandals are selected. One is Puthalapattu mandal. Which is developed and another is Pakala mandal. Which is moderately developed.

The selection of these two mandals was based on development indicators. The indicators chosen are the existence of facilities like drinking water, pucca road, medical facilities, agriculture land etc.

The field data collected through a structured interview schedule, keeping in view the fact that the respondents were both illiterates and literates. The Interview schedule based on the objectives of the study. Apart from this schedule, field observations, informal talks with FFWP beneficiaries and discussion with officials and non-officials have also been utilized for enriching the study. In addition to the above, secondary data have been collected from books, journals, circulars, reports, etc. The data were analyzed and presented in a systematic manner.

This study is beset with certain limitations as any other evaluation study of government programmes. The researcher, given his social science background was not able to evaluate the technical and economic aspects of the house holds selected for the study.

The respondents were busy in day to day agriculture activities but were able to give adequate time to the researcher to make a detailed enquiry about FFWP.

The sample of respondents selected for the study is 8 villages. Though food for work programme has been spread throughout the mandal of the district, the study has a limited coverage.

With regard to the field work, inspite of taking prior appointment with officials of the programme, the researcher faced problems like the non-accessibility of the FFWP officials, which resulted, in not gathering full information. Any suggestions and criticism will be createful welcomed and acknowledged.

Dr. G. Thulasiram

Acknowledgement

I deem it a great privilege to express my profound, gratitude to my most revered research supervisor *Dr. B.V. Muralidhar, M.A., M.Phil, Ph.D., Prof. Department of Political Science and Public Administration,* Sri Venkateswara University, Tirupati who took keen interest and encouraged me a great deal in completing this work successfully in time.

I express my warm thanks to Prof. V. Chandramouliswara Rao, Head, Department of Political Science and Public Administration, Prof. A. Balaramaiah, Chairman, BOS, and other Faculty members for their valuable suggestions.

I thank Sri B. Sudhakar who has spared his valuable time to help me in completion of the research work. I take this opportunity to thank the faculty of other Departments and Sister Universities for timely help in completing this work.

I am extremely thankful to all the officials of the Collectorate Office Chittoor District., Chittoor D.R.D.A. Office, C.E.O. Office, Z.P.T.C. Office, Director I.C.S.S.R. Hyderabad. Osmania University Staff, Central University Librarian & Staff, N.I.R.D. Staff & Librarian, Cess & Staff, Ministry of Rural Development & Staff, SERP & Staff for providing me with the necessary information, data and sparing their time to discuss various aspects of the study.

I am grateful to Prof. Sukhadev Thorat Chairman U.G.C. New Delhi, who has provided me with financial assistance in the form of Rajiv Gandhi National Fellowship for research purpose.

I thank my friends Dr. M. Tejomoorthy, Chandraiah, D.Subramanyam, P.B. Reddy, Narasimhulu, Gangulappa, Sanjay Kumar, Ravi Prasad, Dr. Subramanyam, Dr. Giri Babu, Jayachandra, Srinivasulu, Koteswara Rao, Sankar and Mahesh.

I thank P. Murali, B. Krishna Kumari, M. Dhana Sekhar, G. Balaji and *Murali Karthik Computer Center* for their neat typing of the manuscript.

I am greatly indebted to my beloved parents Sri G.Irigaiah, and Smt. G. Manikyamma for their warmth affection constant encouragement completion of the dissertation.

I fail in my duty if I do not acknowledge the unstint support of my beloved brothers Doraswamy, Bala Subramanyam, Balaji, Prasad, Guna Sekhar and sister Chinnari Soujanya for their never failing services for completion of this research work under reference.

G. Thulasi Ram

Contents

Introduction

In India as in any other Third world country, the process of rural planning and development was initiated in the early fifties. Over the years, the approach to rural development has undergone perceptible innovations concomitant with the political and socio-economic transformation in the country. It is natural that in a country, where about three-fourths of the total population is living in the rural area, this sector should gain special significance. It was fully realised that the future of India rests on the prosperity of its rural population. Added to it tidal, waves of distress, migration from rural areas to urban centers left no option to improve the economic condition and quality of life of the rural masses.

The country faces several natural calamities like drought and floods, which result in the fall in agricultural production. Rural sector is extremely backward and weak. The farmer's class has mostly remained deprived of the development benefits for want of resources. The pace of development among the different states of the country and within the state, and among regions within the districts has not been uniform. There are not only regional differences, but the divide appears to be ever widening. There are still districts which fall short of basic infrastructural facilities and employment opportunities. It is from these district tales of starvation deaths from time to time, massive migration of labour is reported. Therefore, it is quite imperative that such districts are to be identified and a sincere attempt is to be made to bring them on par with other districts.

The Planning Commission has identified 150 most backward districts of the country on the basis of prevalence of poverty indicated by SC/ST population, agricultural productivity per worker and agricultural wage rate. Most of them happen to be tribal districts. There is need for substantial additional investment in these districts to convert their surplus labour into the required capital formation solving livelihood issues.

Floods, drought, unemployment and poverty for a long time have been the plaguing problems of rural India. The climatic diversities and heavy dependence of Indian agriculture on monsoon are interlinked with these problems. It has been observed that always in other parts of the country, people face famine conditions created by the natural disasters. Although the situation has changed since the beginning of the planning era, emphasis was laid on irrigation and, later, technological changes in agriculture increased the overall production, but still the major part of crop lands in the country are in the grip of natural calamities.

On the other side, ours being predominantly an agricultural country, the agriculture sector had always a major role in providing gainful employment to the labour force. Unfortunately, there are large number of persons, especially amongst the weaker sections (Marginal and Small Farmers and Agricultural Labourers), who suffer from seasonal, disguised and chronic unemployment in the country. Although eradication of poverty and unemployment has been one of the main goals of planning in India, in spite of government's efforts, the situation is worsening and unemployment is posing a great threat to the general economy and social well being of the nation every year generally.

Labour incentives, rural public workers have been accorded an important role in the development process since the formative period of modern development theories and policies, because they offer the opportunity to pursue simultaneously the objective of employment creation and capital formation. A potentially important role for food aid in supporting public works was also identified early on. Since the 1960's and early 1970's a range of programmes has been evolved from relief works in emergency situations through seasonal programmes aimed at supplementary wage employment to those with emphasis mainly on the long term creation of assets.

The economic policies of the government are in the nature of a frontal attack on the problems of poverty and mass unemployment, particularly in the rural areas. The primacy given by the government to rural development is reflected in raising the total outlay in the Sixth Plan, covering the period 1978-83 for rural development to about 43 per cent as against 37.5 per cent in the fifth plan period. India continues to be basically a rural country and rural development of a just and balanced kind is needed not only to wipe out the grosser forms of poverty, but also for the country's political stability. The objectives of rural development may broadly be defined as maximizing production in agriculture and allied activities in the rural areas, generating maximum possible employment opportunities, especially for the vulnerable sections of the community, so as to enable them to improve their standard of living and provide them certain basic amenities like drinking water, health care, and education. Any such programme must ensure maximum use of local resources, both human and material physical adoption of appropriate technology that can suit the people and local involvement in planning and implementation of programme.

Broadly speaking, the strategy of rural development has been designed to improve the economic and social life of a specific group of people the rural poor. It involves extending the benefits of development to the poorest among those who seek for a livelihood in the rural areas. Thus, in all the programmes of rural development, special attention is paid to schemes benefiting especially the weaker sections of the community like small and marginal farmers, share-croppers and tenants, and landless agricultural labourers with the main objective of providing full employment.

The All India Rural Credit Review Committee in its report warned if the fruits of development continue to be denied to the large section of rural community, while prosperity accrues to some, tensions social and economic may not only upset the process of orderly peaceful change in the rural economy, but even frustrate the nation's efforts to set up agriculture production. It was, therefore, necessary to make arrangement for the distribution of fruits of development to the rural weak and backward sections of society. All development efforts center round the human prosperity. The basic needs of human beings were like food, shelter, clothing, health, education and the opportunity for employment. Any process of growth that does not fulfil these needs is a negation of the idea of development. Thus, development is mainly concerned with economic well-being or ability to create facilities for proper growth of societies.

Rural development has recently become a fashionable slogan for national governments and theorists on rural development have begun to evaluate the rural India with its problems of poverty, landed aristocracy, caste hegemony and exploitation of weaker sections by politically powerful elements. Similarly practitioners involved in rural reconstruction also began to analyze the causes of poor response to the programmes of rural development, such as rapid growth of population, rigid caste and class systems, extreme poverty, illiteracy, powerful vested interests, dependence on government support and lack of organizations of the rural poor.

To achieve the objectives of rural development, several programmes were under taken. New approaches were adopted and experimental or pilot projects were launched in the past. The well-known among them were the Sriniketan Experiment of Tagore (1920), Braynes Guragaon (1920), Rural Re-construction Project in Baroda (1932), Fikra Development Scheme in Madras (1946) and the Etawah Pilot Project in U.P. (1948). India is predominantly an agricultural country and its 80 per cent population lives in rural areas with farming as their main occupation. In terms of methods of production social organization and political mobilization rural sector is extremely backward and weak in the field of agriculture have increased the gap between the rich and the poor. As the better off farmers adopted modern farm technology and structural and institutional changes, the farmers class has mostly remained deprived of the development benefits for want of resources political influence and right approach.

According to the latest below poverty line (BPL) survey rural population, it consists mainly of the underprivileged segments scheduled castes, scheduled tribes, muslims and the artisan castes. Poverty, which is identified with the slum dwellers in urban sector, is growing day by day, because of the movement of the people belonging to socially marginal groups from the countryside. During the post independence period, it is true that certain weaker sections, for example, the scheduled castes have been the target groups under various rural development and wage employment programmes. Therefore, it is necessary to have an overall view of the incidence of poverty at all India level. The review pertaining to the performance of the anti-poverty programmes is also incorporated for understanding limitations of the wage employment programmes intended for reducing the rural poverty. Agricultural and non-agricultural development till the closing years of the decade of sixties did not make any significant impact with regard to the alleviation of rural poverty. The government started getting increasingly concerned seriously with rural poverty and began to contemplate adoption of suitable measures to strengthen process of alleviation of rural poverty.

The rural economy is severely affected when drought occurs, successive droughts can shatter the fragile economy to the extent that it takes a considerable time to recuperate. Drought brings in its train shortage of fodder and drinking water for life stock. Subsidiary activities such as milk production of live stock based commodities, show a sudden downswing. The effect is particularly severely felt in the western parts of the country where the livestock based economics are predominant. However, animal husbandry is important subsidiary activity, particularly for small and marginal farmers all over the country and the effect of drought will be severe on this subsidiary sector.

A permanent solution to the problems of poverty, under-employment and unemployment can be found in the framework of a rapidly expanding economy the long term strategy of poverty eradication, the government has taken specific steps to ensure the development of drought prone, desert, tribal and hill areas and similar other backward areas. In addition, there are schemes for dispersal of industries to backward regions. Such dispersal of industries is promoted through the grant of investment and transport subsidies conversional finance.

It would be seen that growth oriented development is a necessary precondition for eradication of poverty. All that promotes economic development is being viewed in this perspective. As a broad policy postulates it is believed that all programmes for the development of rural areas are contributing substantially to the alleviation of poverty. The ultimate objective is to improve the quality life of the rural poor. Thus, quality can be imparted to the life style of the poor mainly through an augmentation in their incomes. Such an income increase is planned to be brought about through the increased opportunities for employment and production.

Rural India is real India. Rural areas account for nearly three fourths of the population of the country and have much larger concentration of people below the poverty line. Small size of land holdings, poverty, unemployment underemployment, starvation, malnutrition, ill-health, illiteracy, ignorance, idleness, less mobility of labour, casteism, exploitation by vested interests, low productivity, unorganized sector etc., some of the features of rural areas in India· (Mahatma Gandhi wrote "if you went to the village of India, you will see utter half starved skeletons and living corpses"). Poverty and unemployment are the twin problems that confront the rural sector. An analysis of the 43rd round survey of National Sample Survey Organization (1987-88) revealed that a little over 90 per cent of the rural poor live below poverty line in the 10 major states.

Most of the country's labour force is in rural area. About 58 per cent of the labour force is self-employed, most in agriculture activities. Only about 12 per cent of the increase in the labour force is absorbed in the organized sector. Only 15.8 per cent of the workers are engaged in regular wage paid employment and 25.9 per cent are casual labour. Unemployment is still a burning problem in India. Particularly, in rural areas unemployment is more in the nature of underemployment. It is varying degrees consisting those who are prepared to work for their livelihood. Normally, employment for some days is available in family agricultural operations. But such labour is highly unremunerative. An overwhelmingly larger proportion of the total labour force is employed as agricultural workers.

It is well-known fact that rural India is plagued by the problem of high level of surplus labour. This surplus labour is manifest not so much in open unemployment as the form of underemployment and disguised unemployment. Some of the people migrate from rural areas to urban areas. The phenomenon of underemployment by implication would mean that the employment opportunities that are available are not productive in the sense of ensuring adequate returns or earning to the workers in developing economics unemployment to a great extent is structural. The demand for labour is less and employment opportunities are limited over to the shortage of capital equipment and other complementary resources. Unemployment and under employment are of entirely different in nature.

The programme had succeeded, to some extent, in creating a viable infra-structure in the rural areas including the extension machinery. The second plan strategy for mitigating unemployment suffered from inherent contradiction. In its employment chapter it strongly advocated the adoption of labour intensive techniques of production. It talked of creating a milieu for the small man even in the Second Five Year Plan, which placed relatively more emphasis on the creation of gainful employment opportunities. It was felt that the problem of unemployment, especially in an under-developed country like ours, could be solved after a period of intensive development. The same view point of treating employment as by product of development, persisted among the planning elite. The country even during the Third Five Year Plan period, when the problem of unemployment had become acute. The Third plan target of 14 million employment opportunities included an estimate of 3.5 million employment opportunities in agriculture on the basis of physical targets of additional area brought under irrigation, soil conservation land reclamation and schemes of similar nature. On the assumption that employment opportunities in agriculture during 1966-71 would be of the order of about 4.5 million, an employment potential of 20 to 21 million was envisaged during the Third plan period.

Unemployment in varying degrees of intensity has always been a problem and the root cause of poverty in India. Removal of hunger and unemployment along with the provision of a richer and more varied life to the people has been the major goals of Indian planning. The basic belief was that economic growth would generate sufficient employment to absorb the additional labour force coming into the labour market, plus the backlog. In the early days of the planning much faith was placed in the percolation effect of economic growth. But this by itself does not lead to an automatic increase in employment opportunities. At the end of each five-year Plan, the number of unemployed persons has been more than in the beginning.

Unemployment in India manifests itself in rural India. Apart from normal sectional plans, several special programmes like rural works programme, Rural Manpower Programme (RMP), Cash Scheme for Rural Employment (CSRD), Pilot Intensive Rural Employment Programme (PIRDP), Food For Work Programme (FFWP) were launched to solve the problems of unemployment and under-employment and thus eliminate poverty. But all these have failed to create any significant impact in improving the socio-economic conditions of the rural masses. The Sixth plan admitted that it failed, in the field of employment, and that the picture has been so far from satisfactory and the number of unemployed and underemployed have actually gone up. The strategy consisted of launching of programmes like Integrated Rural Development Programme (IRDP), National Rural Employment Programme (NREP) and Rural Landless Employment Guarantee Programme (RLEGP) for specific target groups for employment creation, income generation and poverty alleviation. The IRD programme was launched in 1978-79 with the primary objective of raising the poorest families in rural areas above the poverty line by giving them income generating assets and providing them access to credit and other inputs.

Employment

It has been observed that more and more construction works have been taken under the FFWP employment provided under the programme. It is important to keep in mind that, by and large, earth works are completed whereas building works linger. For periods varying between 2 to15 months in building work the beneficiaries of the sample, by and large, did not get employment for more than two weeks at a time. This is due to sarpanch's is lack of interest in the work and as a consequence works were taken in different periods resulting in the change of composition of labourers. Another reason in daily of work is non-availability of grant in time and some times material is not available in remote areas as well.

The labourers getting employment three to six weeks were mostly from earth works like road repairs, ancient tube well repairs etc. The position of building workers was worse because of the material component problem of allotment rate of skilled working. The work under the programme was very attractive from the point of view short term employment.

Owing to tight position of food grain stocks, the quantity of food grains to be given to workers under the programme has been 5 kgs per head per day for smooth implementation of the programme. It is necessary that food grains distributed to the workers, are readily available at a nearby place where from it could be made without delay. For this purpose, the state government has been directed to build up their own stocks of coarse food grains (other than rice and wheat). It emphasis that the food grains to be distributed under the programme should be in accordance with the eating habits of the local people. Local procurement of food grains minimizes the difficulties of transportation and ensures timely supply to the wage earners. It has been reiterated that the works to be executed under the programme durable, and should not be below the minimum specification approved by the technical experts. Wherever the standards and specification for any category of works they have not been laid down for the approval of the technical authorities concerned. In this regard it has to be obtained before executing the works on the basis of Master plan for development of the area which is readily available all the time. It would be easier to take up works under the FFWP depending on the availability of quantity of food grains and the priority to be given to each items of work.

Another point which need urgent attention is distribution of food grains to the labourers employed in the works taken up under the programme. It may be mentioned that there have been number of complaints of leakage and malpractice's in the course of distribution of food grains under the programme. It has come to notice that some times the full quantity of food grains to which a worker is entitled is not received by him. Also the payment of wages on kind is delayed at times considerably because of the delay in bringing food grains to the work sites for the workers. The need for streamlining the monitoring system can also be hardly over-emphasized. There have been complaints regarding misutilisation of food grains and malpractices creeping into the programme. The arrangements distribution of food grains had not only varied from state to state, but even district to district within a state. There is, therefore, a need to streamline method. At present the empty bags costing several thousands of rupees retained by the distributing agencies like contractors of fair price shops. These may be handed over to the village panchayats to augment their income, which could be used for the purchase of material like bricks, cement etc. Some of the panchayats sell food grains to meet such expenditure at present.

Fair price shops and village panchayats were the most important agencies responsible for the distribution of food grains. Nearly 65 per cent selected beneficiaries had claimed that the agencies responsible for distribution food grains were located within the village where the villagers had to go out to collect their share of food grains.

To majority of the selected beneficiaries, the food grains were distributed either through coupon system or muster rolls. Nearly 79 per cent of the beneficiaries were satisfied with the present system of distribution of food grains followed in their villages. Those who were not satisfied with the system of distribution gave delay payment in adequate stocks “Center is not in the village” and crowd at fair shops as the main reasons of their distribution. The main suggestion put forward for making improvement in the existing system of distribution be made at work site and assortment of work may be done daily and weekly, stocks of food grains for payment should be made in full at one time and number of shops distributing food grains increased.

The government has appointed specific staff to deal with FFWP. The work has been managed by utilizing the services of the existing staff by readjustment. It is suggested that suitable strengthening at appropriate levels should be done for efficient handling of the programme including its monitoring and progress reporting.

Out of 80 selected villages, only 50 per cent reported having received quality food grains. In the remaining villages, it was reported satisfactory or bad efforts should be made to see that good quality food grains are supplied to the workers. Nearly 78 per cent of the selected beneficiaries reported that the quality of food grains supplied was good. The UPA government introduced National Rural Employment Guarantee Act (NREGA). This will provide a legal guarantee for atleast 100 days of employment, to begin with, as an asset creating public works programmes every year at minimum wages programme for at least one able bodied person in every rural, urban poor and lower-middle class household should get benefited.

The government on the advice of the national advisory council is bringing forth Rural Employment Guarantee Act before the Parliament. The main features of the proposed act are as follows:

(1) Every household in rural India atleast adult member will have a right for atleast 100 days of guaranteed employment every year. The employment will be in the form of the manual labour at the statutory minimum wage and the wages shall be paid within 7 days of the week during which works were done.

(2) Work should be providing within 15 days of demanding it and the work should be located within 5 kilometers distance of the labour residence.

(3) If work is not provided to anybody with in the given time, he/she will be paid a daily unemployment allowance, which will be at least one third of the minimum wages.

(4) Workers employed on public works will be entitled to medical treatment and hospitalization in case of injury at work along with the daily allowance of the statutory minimum wage in case of death or disability of a worker an exgratia payment shall be made to his legal heirs as per provisions of the workmen compensation act.

(5) Five per cent of wages may be deducted as contribution to welfare schemes like health insurance; survivor's benefits maternity benefits, in the case of female labours and social security schemes.

(6) For transparency and accountability all accounts and records of the programme will be made available for public scrutiny.

(7) For non-compliance with rules strict penalties have been laid down.

(8) The district collector/chief executive officer will be responsible for the programme at the district level. The grama sabha will monitor the works of the grama panchayats by way of social audit.

Government of India (GoI) measures aimed at creation of employment opportunities during the planning period. The central objective of economic planning was to initiate a process of development, which would raise living standard and create new opportunities for richer than more varied life in the early years of planners in India maximization employment opportunity was not considered to be an important objective in itself, employment generation was looked upon as by-product of the economic growth. It was clearly stated First Five Year Plan that full employment was not an end in itself and should be regarded as corollary of development rather than as a direct objective.

Foremost consideration was given in the First plan to the rural sector for tackling the problems of unemployment, mainly because of the magnitude and seriousness of its problem. Expansion in rural employment opportunities, would also relieve the pressure on urban employment. The Community Development Programme (CDP) launched in 1952 addressed itself more to decentralization of development effort, besides adding a development dimension to administration.

The five-year plans adopted employment generation as an important goal of economic planning. But since employment was until recently treated as a derivative of growth, the plan strategy did not make much dent on the unemployment problems. Since launching of the Fifth Plan a direct attack had been made on unemployment as was done in the case of poverty. As a result, a number of specific wage and self-employment generation schemes have been formulated and implemented. Apart from promoting the infrastructure for improving productivity and social development in rural areas, a strategy to reach the poor section of society through programmes of asset building, income generation, and wage employment has been evolved over successive plan periods. This process culminated in a frontal attack on poverty with high level of investment during the Eighth Plan. The strategy of poverty alleviation has centered on a package of programme under major streams *viz.*

1. Self-employment Programme and
2. Wage employment Programme.

The Sixth Plan laid emphasis on strengthening the socio-economic infrastructure in rural areas under IRDP aiming at reduction of disparities. The Seventh Plan emphasized on creating new employment opportunities special programmers for income generation, participation of people at the grass roots level. The Eighth Plan emphasis on building up of rural infrastructure priority for rural roads with the focus on tribal, hill and desert areas minor irrigation, soil conversation, social forestry and participation of people in rural development programmes. The centre announced new welfare package to the poorer section of society to bring them into the main streams of national life in 1995. Launched on Independence Day 1995, the package has become a new strategy for rural development the component of the package the national social assistant scheme will provide old age pension. Survivor benefits Million House Scheme, pre and post natal assistance for mother and premium subsidy for group life insurance all targeted at families below the poverty line. The second component package the midday meal would be extended throughout the country for school children priority to agriculture and rural development with a view to generating adequate productive employment and eradication of poverty is one of the objectives of the Ninth Five Year Plan.

To alleviate poverty and generate employment to the rural people government launched a number anti-poverty programmes. A brief review of the Rural Employment Generation Programmes is as follows.

After Independence about 32 Programmes for rural development have been introduced for the reduction of poverty and well being of the rural weak. These programmes are in the First Five Year Plan, Community Development Programme (CDP) (1952) and National Extension Scheme (NES) (1953). In the Second Five Year Plan, Khadhi and Village Industries (1957), Multipurpose Tribal Development

Blocks (MTDB) (1959), Package Programme and Intensive Agriculture District, Development Programme (IADDP) (1960). In the Third Five Year Plan, Applied Nutrition Programme (ANP) (1962), Intensive Agriculture Area Development Programme (IAADP) (1964), High Yielding Variety Programme (HYVP) (1966), Farmers Training Education (FTE) (1966), well Construction Programme (1966), Rural Work Programme (RWP) (1967), Tribal Development Block (TDB) (1968), Rural Manpower Programme (RMP) (1969) and Composite Programme For Women and Pre-School-Going Children (1969). In the Fourth Plan, Drought Prone Area Programme (DPAP) (1970), Crash Scheme For Rural Employment (CSRE) (1971), Small Farmers Development Agency (SFDA) (1971), Tribal Area Development Programme (TADP) (1972), Pilot Project Tribal Development (PPTD)(1972), Pilot Intensive Rural Employment Programme (PIREP) (1972), Minimum Needs Programme (MNP) (1972), Command Area Development Programme (CADP) (1974). In the Fifth Five Year Plan, Hill Area Development Programme (HADP) (1975), Food For Work Programme (FFWP) (1977), Desert Development Programme (DDP) (1977), Whole Village Development Programme (WVDP) (1979), Training Rural Youth For Self Employment (1979), Integrated Rural Development Programme (IDDP) (1979), and in the Seventh Five Year Plan, National Rural Employment Programme (NREP) (1980) and Development of Women And Children in Rural Areas (DCRA) (1983), Jawahar Rozgar Yojana (JRY) (1989), National Food For Work Programme (NFFWP) (2002), National Rural Employment Guarantee Act (NREGA) (2005). Besides the governments efforts, it has become a general belief that in the early planning periods the welfare and development programmes sponsored by the central and state governments had benefited only the better off sections of the rural society. Thus, realizing the magnitude of the problems of the rural people and especially of the weaker section, the centre as well as state government launched several programmes during the Fourth Five-year Plan period to eradicate poverty and unemployment.

The programmes like Small Farmers Development Agency (SFDA), Marginal Farmers and Agriculture Labourer's (MFAL), Drought Prone Area Programme (DPAP), Crash Scheme for Rural Employment (CSRF), Pilot Intensive Rural Employment Project (PIREP), Employment Guarantee Scheme (EGS), Integrated Rural Development Antyodaya aimed at creating employment and livelihood opportunities to small and marginal farmers and agricultural labourers in tribal areas dry and drought prone areas of the country.

Targeted group oriented programmes under the targeted area approach, and intra-regional imbalances the benefits of development were sought to be corrected through area specific development programmes enumerated in the foregoing lines. Under the target group approach and intra-socio-economic group imbalances were sought to be corrected by a couple of group specific programmes called the scheme for the Small Former Development Agency (SFDA), Marginal Farmers and Agricultural Labourers Schemes (MFALS) during (1970-71).

The growth oriented approaches were not able to tackle the problem of rural poverty and unemployment as expected. The large farmers and dominant groups derived the benefits of these development programmes. The technological changes that have taken place in the agriculture sector were to have contributed to the widening income inequalities and disparities it was felt that there was a need to specially design the programmes suitable to different target groups as small and marginal farmers and landless labourers who constitute the bulk of the rural poor.

Rural Employment Programme-Implementation and Objectives

1. The orientation in these guidelines is to provide wage employment to every person seeking employment with

in the area he/she is residing. The effect is to reduce the need for unusual migration of labour due to the adverse conditions from the affected villages.

2. The district collector should canvas meeting of the entire department including NGO's and identify the works, village-wise the scheme-wise where labour component is involved for selecting works.
3. The district collector shall endeavor to ensure that at least one work is to be commenced in each habitation, as indicated by the planning department under Janmabhoomi Programme, to avoid hardship local workers in view of the drought and to avoid migration.
4. As and where there is need, a second or third work can also be commenced.
5. To this effect funds available under different schemes of all the departments/localbodies/committees/NGO's/government/agencies/corp-oration shall be worked out and still if any gap is existing, the district collector may send necessary proposals to the government for all allocation of funds.

Self Employment Programme

Programmes launched during the Fourth Plan on the recommendations made by the rural credit review committee (1969). The activities taken up under this programme include identification of eligible small farmers. Identification of their problem formulation of suitable programmes, arranging supply of various inputs helping the small farmers in securing institutional loans arrangement of marketing facilities. This programme was merged with IRDP in 1980. The Marginal Farmers and Agriculture Labourers agency (MFALA) was also set up along with SFDA to assist the marginal farmers in taking up productive activities like horticulture animal husbandry, dairing etc., and helping the marginal farmers in securing institutional credit and other social consumption designed to assist in raising consumption levels of those living below the poverty line and thereby to improve productive efficiency of the people. The programme is essentially an investment in human resources, the basic needs of the people identified for this programme are elementary education, adult education, rural water supply, rural roads, rural electrification, rural housing environment and nutrition, during the Seventh Plan it was proposed to integrate this programme with anti-poverty programmes.

Crash Scheme for Rural Development Programme

(CSRDP) it was introduced during the year 1971-72 as non-plan programme and later it was upgraded as a central plan programme. The basic objective of the programme was to generate employment in productive rural works creating 1000 mandays of employment in each district in a day and on an average of 2.50 lakh mandays of employment should be generated in every district.

Pilot Insentive Rural Employment Programme

(PIREP) which was implemented in 15 selected blocks in October 1972 for a period of three years was basically an action cum-research project to provide employment to all those offering their services for a wage through execution of work project for the creation of durable assets of a continuing nature to explore the possibility of imparting new skills to some workers and assisting them finding continuous employment in the secondary and territory sectors in the rural and urban areas it also aimed at studying of the problems of unemployment among wage seeking rural workers. The scheme was expected to provided employment to at least 1000 persons in a year in every district and employment to one person in a family in which no one was employed. The programme was to cover a variety of agro-climatic zones. The works to be taken are soil conservation, minor irrigation, farm forestry water conservation and ground water recharging pisci-culture tank, pasture development, rural godowns, roads, rural water supply, school buildings, houses for weaker section. The wage and non-wage component under the programme was fixed at 60:40.

Employment Guarantee Scheme

Besides, the wage employment programmes sponsored by the union government and implemented by the state government under its direction.

The Employment Guarantee Scheme (EGS) was formulated as a regular scheme on the basis of experiences gained in the working of pilot scheme undertaken in the seriously drought districts in the state in the last sixties and early years of the decade of seventies to deal with the problems rural underemployment and unemployment it supplements other regular employment generating programmes in action. Since 1975-76 when it was expanded to function on state wise basis. The number of mandays generated by and large investment made in it have been going up. It provides guarantee of employment to all the needy adults men and women, in the rural areas of the state. This guarantee is unlimited and is neither constrained by the seize of the landholding or any other assets or by income of the person asking for employment only the person concerned has to be willing to undertake physical work. There are no restrictions as regard the number of persons from each family who wish to be employed. Employment under this scheme is available through out the year. There is no constraint in regard to the total number of employment opportunities for the poor and for systematic strengthening of the local infrastructure, soil improvement or minor irrigation (or) school building as the supportive factor in the development process.

Drought Prone Area Programme

Drought Prone Area Programme (DPAP) formulated the resource based or problems based development approach. It sought to reduce the severity of the impact of drought in rain dependent rural areas, stabilize income of the people particularly that of the weaker section of the community. It sought to restore ecological balance through development and management of water resource soil and moisture as well.

Wage Employment Generation Programmes

Rural Man Power Programme

Towards the close of 1960-61 the Rural Man Power Programme (RMPP) was taken up in 32 community development blocks on a pilot basis with the object of providing employment 100 days at least 2.5 million persons by the last year of the Third Plan, particularly in areas exposed to pronounced seasonal unemployment and under employment. For the programme which covered 1,000 CD blocks, by the end of the originally contemplated outlay of Rs.150 crores could be provided due to resource constrains nevertheless, it generated 137 million man days of employment until 1968-69, the year in which the programme was terminated.

Rural Works Programme

During 1970-71 the rural works programme (RMP) was launched in 54 selected district of 13 states which were identified as drought prone on the basis of well defined norms. Such as extent of irrigated area quantity and distribution of rainfall and high frequency of drought, with the objective of mitigating gradually the severity of scarcity condition in this area. In terms of population and geographical areas the programme covered 600 lakhs or 12 per cent of population and 5.65 SG kms or about 20 per cent of the area in the country respectively the object was sought to be achieved through taking up of schemes of long term productive nature in areas prone to recurrent drought and providing employment opportunities to the people in these identified areas. The programme focused mainly on the execution of rural works such as medium and minor irrigation soil conservation and forestation, road building, drinking water supply and generation of employment opportunities through these rural works.

In the light of the midterm appraisal of Fourth Five Year Plan, the reports of the task force for integrated rural development programme setup by the Planning Commission in October 1971. The strategy of development under the RWP underwent a change, after releasing the development of drought prone areas demand long time measures, and the need for a comprehensive programme in the direction restoration of the proper ecological balanced and optimum, utilizations of land, water, live stock and human resource. Accordingly 1973 the programme was re-oriented with an area development approach, and redesign as the drought prone area programme.

Food for Work Programme

The government has accumulated a buffer stock of over million tones of food grains in 1977. A suggestion was made by several economists that the surplus food grains be used as payment for work to the person living below the poverty line. Consequently, the FFWP was conceived the main objectives of the programme

1. To generate additional gainful employment for both men and women in rural areas.
2. To create durable community assets and the strengthen the social infrastructure in order to increase production and raise living standard in rural areas and to utilize surplus food grains for the development of the country human resource.

Thus, the government decided to use the food grains as a payment for the labour rendered in the execution of specific projects. The central government allocated 27 lakhs tones of food grains for the FFWP during 1979-80 out of 22.3 lakh tonnes provided to the state government upto 31st December 1979, only 11.9 lakh tonnes were utilized. This indicated an overall utilization of about only 50 per cent. Which was disappointing; it is widely held the state government being preoccupied with problems of political destabilization not able to take the advantage of the scheme. In an-overall review of the programme, it was revealed that out of 20 districts market wages of agriculture labourers improved only in two districts. Thus, by and large, the programme did not make any impact on wages. This was due to the fact that the magnitude of the programme was too small to make such an impacts on the whole, it becomes apparent that the impact of different employment programmes in the rural sector had been at these programmes were adhoc in nature. They proved relief measures rather than providing permanent solution to the problems of unemployment and poverty. Besides, they were not dovetailed able to the area specific rural development programmes. Rural unemployment under employment affects the poor in the rural areas more intensely and has been the major cause for high incidence of poverty in rural areas. One of the major objectives of Sixth Five Year Plan adopted two pronged strategy towards eradication of poverty and unemployment was redistribution of income and consumption on favour of the poor people in the rural areas by significantly increasing employment opportunities in the rural areas through creation of self-employment opportunities under IRDP and some other areas and or skill development programmes reflected in the plan. Wage employment opportunities under national rural employment programmes and rural landless employment guarantee programme.

National Rural Employment Programme

The FFWP was restricted and redesigned as National Rural Employment Programme (NREP) from October,1980 and become regular programme in the Sixth Plan 1st April, 1981 to wage an assault on rural poverty NREP was implemented as centrally sponsored programme with 50 per cent central assistance. Additional employment of the order of 300-400 million man-days per year for the unemployed and under-employed was envisaged under the NREP.

The major objectives of the programme are:

1. Generation of additional gainful employment for the unemployed and underemployed persons both men and women in rural areas.
2. Creation of productive community assets for direct and continuing benefits to the poverty groups and for strengthening rural economic and social infrastructure, which will lead to rapid growth of rural economy and steady rise in the levels of the rural poor.
3. Improvement in the overall quality life in the rural areas.

Progress of the NREP under the Sixth Plan revealed that as against an allocation of Rs. 1,620 crores actual expenditure both by the central and state government was of the order of Rs. 1,834 crores. There was, however, a decline in food grain utilization which was due to several factors such as inadequate arrangement of distribution, availability of food grains at a lower price in the open market to issue price preference of workers for coarse grains rather than wheat/ rice which is supplied under NREP, keeping this in view the government decided to distribute food grains at subsidized rate from January 16, 1984. Despite this, there was only marginal improvement of food grains utilization during 1984-1985 the employment generation under NREP was 1.775 million man days as against the target of 1500-2000 million man days during the Sixth Plan.

Review of the progress of NREP during the first four years of the Seventh Plan reveals that Rs. 2,940 crores was spent during 1985-86 and 1988-89. But as against it, the employment generated was of the order of 1,477 million man-days. In other words, while more funds have been furnished into the programme, commensurate increase in employment generation has not come about besides this the studies conducted by national institute of rural development, Indian institute of public administration and Gandhi labour institute highlights some of the short comings of the programme. It revealed that employment being provided under the programme is for a very short duration and can not make an impact on the levels of living of the rural people, the wages paid under NREP are often lower than those the remarket wage rates. The selection of the beneficiaries is not proper in as much as the poorest of the poor whom the programme is meant are some times left out altogether.

Rural Landless Employment Guarantee Programme

(RLEGP) It was launched on 15th August, 1983 with objectives as follows:

1. To improve and expand employment opportunities, particularly for the rural landless labour with a view to providing guarantee of employment to at least one member of every rural landless labour household up to 100 days in the year.
2. To create productive and durable assets for direct and continuing benefits to the poor and
3. To improve the overall quality of life in the rural areas.

The programme is funded by the central government on 100 per cent. Resources are allocated to the states on the basis of the prescribed criteria giving 50 per cent of weightage to number of agricultural labourers. Marginal farmers and marginal workers and 50 per cent weightage to incidence of poverty. Contractors are not permitted to be engaged in the execution of works under the programme. The programme includes projects of social forestry Indira Awaas Yojana and million well schemes.

An outlay of Rs.1,744 cores had been earmarked in the central sector under the Seventh Plan. The target was to generate 1,013 million man days of employment during the plan period the progress of RLEGP during the Seventh Plan revealed that during the first four years, sum of Rs. 2,412 crores was utilized and this helped to generate employment to the tune of 1,154 million man days.

The government of India conducted a concurrent evaluation of NREP all over the country 1987-88, which observed that (1) 63 per cent of villages, were covered under NREP. (2) On an average of 91 per cent of employment per work is by unskilled workers and 9 per cent by skilled workers. (3) 39 per cent of the workers belonging to the scheduled castes.16 per cent to the scheduled tribes and the rest of 45 per cent belong to other communities. (4) 16 per cent of the total workers employed were women.

However evaluation studies have revealed that NREP suffered for certain short comings such as :

1. The employment provided under the NREP was for very short duration to the beneficiaries.
2. The elements of proper planning and co-ordination were inadequate.
3. Definite guidelines as to formulation of self-employment generation projects were not issued.
4. The selection of beneficiaries was not proper in as much as the poorest of the poor were at times left out.
5. Infrastructural gaps were not identified before the implementation of the programme.
6. There was no provision for maintenance of the assets created under NREP afforestation, restructuring the cropping pattern and pasture development, changes in the agronomic practices, livestock and dairy development, in the hot and semi arid and dry sub-humid regions located in different parts of the country.

Command Area Development Programme

The Command Area Development Programme (CADP) was based on similar approach like the DPAP it was described as dynamic process of harnessing the rhythm of water (it availability at different parts of time) with the rhythm of crops (their requirement of water) at the crucial stages of emergence, seedling killings, preflowering, flowering, and the rhythm of the soil (its moisture reduction capacity etc.,) water soil and crops have to be orchestrated by the Command Area Development Agency (CADA). Its objectives was to maximize utilization of the limited resources of land and water through reduction of loss of water through, extend areas under irrigation and agronomic practice and increase in the intensity of cropping and yield per unit of water and land.

The Programme in India

The schemes aims at directly benefiting the persons in the rural areas who live below the poverty line by providing them with employment and raising their incomes and nutritional levels with comfortable food stocks of 15.4 million tones in 1977 in the country. The FFWP was therefore taken up in April 1977 as an integral part of the strategy for a direct attack on the problems of rural unemployment and poverty. The works executed under the scheme are aimed at to create durable community assets and strengthen the rural infrastructure.

The Union Ministry Rural reconstruction is the co-ordination agency at the central level and have issued detailed guidelines to the state government for planning implementation and monitoring the programme. In the state the programme is administered at three levels namely district block and the village with state level authorities issuing general policy guidelines.

Magnitude of the Programme

During the first year of the programme 1977-78, 204 lakh

tones of wheat was allocated to different states under this programme. The total utilization was about 1.27 lakhs tones. During 1978-79, the food grains released were of the order of 13.9 lakhs tones and the utilization was about 12 lakhs tones of food grain released upto November, 1979 were of the order of 13.61 lakhs tones for the whole year. As per the review prepared by the ministry of rural reconstruction, about 438 lakhs of man days were generated under the programme.

The Scheme of Food For Work Programme

The scheme was introduced in April, 1977 with a three-fold objective, namely, creation of additional employment opportunities in rural areas better maintenance of public works and utilization of surplus food grain stocks. Owing to various constraints inherent in the scheme as originally formulated, the programme did not make much headway initially. The scheme was therefore modified subsequently to include all items of work. This resulted in the creation of durable community assets in addition maintenance of public and community works all type of works like construction various irrigation projects, flood protection and drainage works soil and water conservation, land reclamation projects, afforestation and social forestry works, rural roads, school and dispensary building and panchayat ghars, community centers, drinking water supply scheme deepening and regeneration of tanks and reservoirs irrigation channels, were included under the revised scheme.

The Salient Features of the Modified Schemes

1. Food grains are to be made available to the state governments/union territories(U.T) free of cost for supplementing their budgetary provision for on going plan and non plan schemes, being implemented by state government and taking up new items of capital works as well as for the maintenance and repairs of public works.

2. The food grains are to be utilized for the payment of part of whole of the wages of the labour engaged in the execution of specified works taken up under the scheme
3. Work projects under the scheme can be implemented throughout the year. Till last year, the labour engaged by contractors could also be paid through food grains made available under FFWP provided. It was ensured that the contractors maintained proper accounts and did not misutilise food grains meant to be distributed to the labourers.

The Present Sudy

Owing to the prolonged drought condition for the last 45 years, the importance of FFWP has increased. In some parts of the country, all government planning machinery has been diverted towards the programme. Hence, realizing the importance of this state, it was decided by the government of India to evaluate the programme, particularly from the beneficiary's point of view and its impact and socio-economic condition in the rural areas the task of studying Chittoor District, Andhra Pradesh.

Role of Andhra Pradesh Government in FFWP

1. For the implementation of the scheme, the state government shall prepare an employment guarantee programme within six months of its enactment. The main features to include in the programme are only productive works. That are based economic social and environmental benefits contributing to social equality and have the ability to create permanent assets will be taken up under the programme.
2. The work should be located in rural areas only.
3. When wages are directly linked with the quality of work, they shall be paid according to the schedule of rate fixed by the state government for unskilled

labourers; this schedule shall be so fixed that seven hours of work shall fetch wages equal to the statutory minimum wage fixed by the state.

However, it has now been decided that the distribution of food grains through contractor's a middlemen's in whatever name may be has been stopped. The state governments/union territories are required to show additionally in their expenditure over and above the provided in their budget for the respective items to the extent of value of the food grains utilized calculated at the prescribed rate.

Panchayat Raj institutions (PRI) like grama panchayats, panchayat samithies and Zilla Parishads (ZP) have been authorized to execute work under FFWP food grains upto 10 tones can be allotted to them for the execution of work by district magistrates at their own levels and till almost end of 3rd quarters of 1978-79 only wheat was being supplied to the state government under this, however now given choice to draw entire quantity food grain released to them either in rice or wheat or both as they wished, it has also been decided to utilize coarse grains under the programme if the same has been procured by the state government as a price support measure available in stock with them.

Employment Poverty Reduction Programmes merged with FFWP

Wage employment programmes for poverty reduction. The National Rural Employment Programme (NREP) and Rural Landless Employment Programme (RLEP), were initiated 1970s, (Sixth and Seventh five year plan) and these were merged Jawahar Rozgar Yojana (JRY), the Jawahar Employment scheme in (1989), JRY through asset creation. JRY was subsequently redesigned in (1999) into the Jawarhar Gram Samrudhi Yojana (JGSY), Jawahar village advancement scheme to convert it into project that was primarily for economic infrastructure creation with employment as a secondary objective.

The centrally sponsored Employment Assurance Scheme (EAS) launched 1993, had objectives similar to the JRY programme in 2001, FFWP launched as component of EAS in some states soon after wards EAS, JGSY, and FFWP merged Sampoorna Grameena Rozgar Yojana (SGRY) the full employment scheme with central budget RRS in 100bn, but it continues to be popularly known as FFWP.

The National Rural Employment Programme (NREP) was merged into Jawahar Rozgar Yojana (JRY), Jawahar Grama Samrudhi Yojana (JGSY), Employment Assurance Scheme (EAS). JGSY merged Sampoorna Grameena Rozagar Yojana (SGRY) Again SGRY was also merged into FFWP as well.

Food For Work Programme

A programme of FFWP was launched in 1977 to provide opportunities of work for the rural poor particular in slack employment periods of the year, which would at the same time create durable community assets. Irrigation facilities have been expanded manifold. With a view to removing regional disparities particularly in less endowed disadvantaged areas, like the hill and tribal areas with the use of surplus food grains available in the buffer stock for payment as wages. The programme designed to secure to the rural areas within a reasonable time frame certain basic amenities in the field of education health, drinking water electrification roads, and house sites. Several economists said that these food grains be used as payment for work to the persons living below the poverty line consequently the FFWP was conceived. Several strategies have been worked out a workable solution but these attempts have only touched the fringe of the problem. FFWP is the latest strategy chalked out by the central government to tackle the problems like low level nutrition in the rural population, unemployment and strengthening of infrastructure. The economic importance attached to this scheme can be seen from the fact that it has already been included in the plan strategy for the coming five years. The title of the programme itself conveys its meaning food is distributed to workers as their wages. The department of rural development, ministry of agriculture explains the genesis of the programme as "livelihood at the very doorsteps of the rural poor. This FFWP is a unique way of providing immediate relief to the needy poor people because it not only meets the food needs of the people but also utilizes their unemployed energies in executing of durable assets of long term economic utility. This programme was started on adhoc basis a non-plan programme 1977-78. The government decided to utilize its food stocks, which had been accumulated as the result of its procurement policy of price incentive to farmers, for creating additional employment and improving rural infrastructure facilities. The distinctive aspect of this programme as to pay a part of the wage in the form of food grains at subsidize rates. This improved the wage rate and the nutrition standard among the workers it also tended to stabilize the food prices in some of the districts. This programme will be effective if they are taken up to meet the needs of the local conditions to reduce the tempo of migration out for employment.

It aimed at creating employment and livelihood opportunities to small and marginal farmers and agricultural labourers in tribal areas, dry areas, drought prone areas of the country. The basic philosophy of FFWP is different from other programmes.

The position of buffer stock of major food grains with the central government for the past few years has been very comfortable and the country is no longer in deficit of food grains. It is, however, an in unbelievable fact that a large section of rural community is still unable to get even a meal a day for want of purchasing power and hence is suffering from malnutrition. The fact that while many public works are to be undertaken to provide various *amentia* and infrastructure facilities to satisfy the minimum needs of the country's population. A large rural force remained unemployed and under fed in spite of food grains reserve in the country. It was suggested that this problem should be solved only if organize a programme for giving full time employment to all the able persons in the rural areas for improving their income and nutrition level by creating durable community assets. This in turn would improve the economic life of the rural poor with the help of available food grains, idle manpower could be deployed to create productive assets by launching a programme of infrastructure development in the rural areas. This could solve not only the problem of unemployment, underemployment and malnutrition and rural development to a great extent. Thus, it was thought that a programme like FFWP can play a vital role in tying up idle labour to development progrmmes in the villages.

The FFWP was visualized as a means of achieving the above duel objectives. The main aim of the programme is to generate gainful employment for the unemployed and underemployed persons and in the process create durable community assets in achieving these objectives it also aimed at the utilization of the surplus food grains for the of human resource in rural areas, as also ensure that the weaker sections were provided with adequate food and nutrition during the off seasons, when food prices rise.

The state of Andhra Pradesh once renowned as the granary of the south, for rice had been established as a prime food provider. However in recent times natural disaster and severe extremes of the weather have devastated the state. These creating vagaries have taken their toll in creating situation of drought and severe food shortage in several areas. The state government, ever alert to the people's needs is striving relentlessly to provide relief and assistance in this hour crisis. The FFWP a notable scheme, has emerged out as a successful to address the problems of food shortage and simultaneously encourage self-employment.

FCI stocks to WFP project from the central pool stocks and when required by them. FCI is working as food bank for world Food Programme Projects in India. When India was deficit of food grains WFP used to get stocks to meet the deficiency through out import.

This programme has been launched by the Prime Minister during 2004 for providing food grains in identified 150 most backward districts of the country the beneficiaries of this programme are labourers engaged by the state government development work. Food grains are given as part of wage under the scheme to the rural poor 5 kgs per manday. More than 5 kgs food grains can be given to the labourers under this programme in exceptional cases subject to minimum of 25 per cent of wages to be paid in cash under this programme food grains issued to states free of cost this scheme mentioned by ministry of rural development.

Under the FFWP during the year 2001-2002 about 18.41 lakh tones of food grains have been released to the drought/flood or natural calamity affected states namely Chhatisgarh, Gujarat, Himachal Pradesh, Maharastra, Orissa, Rajastan, Andhra Pradesh, Karnataka, Kerala, in addition, 1 lakh tones food grains being recommended for release to the flood affected state of Bihar. During the year 2000-01 an amount of Rs. 300 crores was allocated under FFWP about 6 lakh tones of food grains wheat and rice were released to the concerned states except Uttaranchal. The ministry of rural development released an amount of Rs. 300 crores to the DRDA to make payment to the FCI against the actual the programme would be implemented centrally sponsored scheme on cost sharing basis between central and state in the ratio 75.25 per cent in the case of union territories the centre would provide the entire 100 per cent funds under the scheme food grains are to be provided free of cost to the state/union territories. The cost of transportation of the food grains from the FCI go down to the work to the work site/PDS and its distribution will be the responsibility of the state governments.

Scope of the FFWP

Poor economic infrastructure and inadequate community assets like roads etc., unemployment and underemployment are well-known in rural areas. Indian farmer otherwise depends heavily on nature for cultivation. Looking at all these aspects, the government of India started this programme in April 1977 it is utilizing the additional stock of food grains available in the country for developmental purpose.

Union Territory governments current levels of expenditure on maintenance of public works in areas is provided under this programme free of cost by central government as an additional to state government, through the Gram vikas vibbag pays for these grains to the Food Corporation of India (FCI) to execute both plan and non-plan schemes and for creation and maintenance of durable community assets in rural areas. These community assets, it is expected, will generate high production and regular income for rural population. The main objective of this scheme is that this programme will utilize the disguised unemployment prevailing in the farm sector by providing the unemployed both food and work in addition to drawing away farm workers whose contribution to agriculture production is negligible, the FFWP would also take care of the landless labourers whose number has swelled in recent years and whose idle energies constitute an important saving potential in the rural areas. This potential can profitably be tapped by giving them appropriate opportunity for employment in constructive activities especially during the inter crop period when they virtually face starvation as no other avenues of remunerative employment are available to them in villages. Thus, it is developmental programme will benefit both rural areas and the rural population.

At the out-set of the programme, its implementation was confined only to a lean period of four months, when farmers and other rural residents sit idle. The farmers in this period were employed in repairs and maintenance of public works. Later on looking at the success of the programme it was extended through out the year.

When certain state governments had expressed their inability in implementing the scheme because of their rural population was accustomed to taking rice, a further modification was introduced under which state government could draw their requirements rice up to 75 per cent of the total quantity. There is a proposal to give option to state governments to have the total requirements of food grains in the forms of wheat or rice according to their choice. It is hoped that this will help rice consuming states to take full advantage of the programme.

The state government extended this scope of the programme to bring under its ambit both plan and non-plan scheme for creation maintenance of durable community assets in rural areas. Now the restrictions apply only to the creation of private and individual assets. The revised list of works under the programme includes following projects; irrigation projects, flood protection works, drainage, anti-water logging works, soil and water conservation, land reclamation works, afforestation and social forestry works, construction of intermediate and field channels, land leveling in the command areas of irrigation projects, roads including state highways, school buildings, panchayat ghars, community centers, drinking water wells and village ponds for providing water for cattle or for developing irrigation and fisheries.

National Rural Employment Guarantee Act (NREGA) scheme will provide a legal guarantee for at least 100 days of employment to begin with on asset creating public work programme every year at minimum wages to at least one able bodies person in every rural and urban poor and lower middle class household. The FFWP is general scheme which can from a part of any scheme of the central or state government being implemented for generation of wage employment in the drought affected districts the programme should be integrated with any and all centrally sponsored scheme state schemes, works taken up by Panchayatraj institutions (PI)/local bodies/government departments/ agencies/corporations/self help groups market committees. Work taken up under clean and green programme will also be covered under the FFWP. The FFWP merged with National Rural Employment Guarantee Act (NREGA) 2005. The basic objective of the act is to enhance livelihood security in rural areas by providing at least 100 days of guaranteed wages employment in a financial year to every household, whose adult members volunteer to do the unskilled manual work. This work guarantee can also serve other objectives generating productive assets, protecting environment empowering rural women, reduction rural urban migration and fostering social equity.

Objectives of the Study

The present study examines the extent to which the objective of the FFWP has been achieved with particular reference to the following:

1. The extent of additional gainful employment generated in the rural areas.
2. The changes income level of the beneficiaries.
3. The contribution of the programme in creating durable community assets and providing infrastructure for rural development.
4. The impact on farm prices and agricultural wages and
5. Impact of the programme on the consumption level and nutritional intake of beneficiaries.

The usefulness of the programme is bringing about the social change in the village community in terms of meeting social obligations, social mobility. It will be seen that while keeping the main objectives of the programme in view, an attempt has been made in the evaluation study to widen the scope of the investigation by including some more items which have relevance larger national objectives.

Methodology

The selected area for the study falls in Chittoor District of Andhra Pradesh. Both primary and secondary data were collected. To study the impact of the FFWP and an empirical study is carried out in the district. Two mandals are selected, one is Puthalapattu mandal, which is developed and another is Pakala mandal, which is moderately developed.

The selection of these two mandals was based on development indicators. The indicators chosen are the existence of facilities like drinking water, pucca road, medical facilities, agriculture land etc.

From Pakala mandal four villages were selected at random for the study. 1. Dasarlapalli 2. Gollapalli 3. Peddabayanapalli 4. Bayanapalli four villages selected from Puthalapattu mandal, 1.Chittipiralla H.W 2. Chittipiralla 3. Nadampalli 4. Sanjeevarayanipalli. Thus the total number of villages covered in present Research study.

The sample beneficiaries of FFWP from each village were selected in proportion to the total number of beneficiaries in the respective villages. On the whole from Puthalapattu mandal 50 sample beneficiaries and from Pakala mandal 50 sample beneficiaries were selected using simple random sampling method.

The field data collected through a structured interview schedule, keeping in view the fact that the respondents were both illiterates and literates. The interview schedule based on the objectives of the study. Apart from this schedule, field observations, informal talks with FFWP beneficiaries and discussion with officials and non-officials have also been utilized for enriching the study. In addition to the above, secondary data have been collected from books, journals, circulars, reports, etc. The data were analyzed and presented in a systematic manner.

Limitations of the Study

1. This study is beset with certain limitations as any other evaluation study of government programmes. The researcher, given his social science background was not able to evaluate the technical and economic aspects of the households selected for the study.
2. The respondents were busy in day to day agriculture activities but were able to give adequate time to the researcher to make a detailed enquiry about FFWP.
3. The sample of respondents selected for the study is 8 villages. Though food for work programme has been spread throughout the mandal of the district, the study has a limited coverage.
4. With regard to the field work, in spite of taking prior appointment with officials of the programme, the researcher faced problems like the non-accessibility of the FFWP officials, which resulted, in not gathering full information.

Review of Literature

(1) D.Murali said that according to the FFWP, the government had earlier cut exercise and customs levies twice for the petroleum products to avoid the price hike, even if it meant a revenue loss of Rs. 4.400 crores.

(2) M. Venugopal Rao, 2004, said that, there was large-scale misuse under food for work programme. According to statistics report of the government, the FFWP being implemented with a massive quantity of 31.5 lakh tones of rice, worth about Rs. 3150 crore, given free of cost by the government of India, and cash of Rs. 990 crore, against 7 lakh workers

sanctioned, as on August 12, 5.83 lakh works were grounded out of which 4.5 lakh works were completed, creating 28.40 crore mandays distributing 26.34 lakh tones of rice to the workers.

(3) Habshi, 2004, says that, as per the guidelines issued by the government, the workers under the FFWP can choose payment of wages per mandays in any of the three option 5 kgs of rice plus Rs. 30 or 8 kgs of rice plus Rs.10 or 10 kgs of rice without any cash component. The selection of works under the FFWP and release of rice were done indiscriminately, and not on the basis of the severity of drought situation.

(4) Lionel Messias, 2003, said that, under the FFWP 5 kgs of food grains per mandays would be given to labourers with minimum of 25 per cent wages in cash. The centre will provide food grains and cash component to the states to generate additional wage employment works relating to water conservation drought proofing and land improvement, flood control and rural connectivity of all-weather roads will be taken up to create wage employment.

(5) Ministry of Rural Development press release, 30-12-2004, FFWP with an allocation of Rs. 2020 crores of each component and 20 lakh of tones of food grains has been launched in 150 districts of the country 14-11-2004. Dr. Manmohan Singh, Prime Minister launched the programme from village Allure in Ranga Reddy District of Andhra Pradesh, Rupees 297.91 crores and 20 lakh tones of food grains have been released as a part of the current year's allocation to 150 districts of the country. The scheme is being funded 100 per cent by the centre. For the states (other than special category states and states in the north-eastern region except Assam) most backward districts have been chosen on the basis of an exercise undertaken by the Planning Commission using three

parameters namely (1). Agricultural productivity (2). Agriculture wage rate and (3) SC/ST population.

(6) Swami Dass Gupta, expressed, that in Andhra Pradesh, 'Food For Work Programme' has been exploited by the corrupt. Analysis says, it would have required huge human power to undertake the 5.77 lakh works clearly the figure was manipulated or the rich misutilised. They also pointed out that instead of using manual labour, as is a condition of the FFWP is many instances excavators were used. The rice should have been released only used the labour component, but there were instances where it was claimed even under the material component.

(7) Ganesh Kumar, Srijith Mishra, 2004, features samachar-institutionalizing corruption through rural job scheme, says that, the most incredible feature of this planned drain of wealth from the productive sector to the underground economy is that no one knows how much is at stake. The conservative estimate is that it will cost Rs. 40,000 crores provide 100 days of alleged work to lakh people, others suggest that the costs could go up to as much as Rs. 1,50,000 crores. The economist Bibek Debroy, whose institutional affiliation does disservice to his professional competence, has even suggested that the cost of servicing NREGA could be around Rs. 2, 80,000 per year, we are not talking loose change; there is serious money involved.

(8) The Indira Gandhi Institute of Development Research, 2004, conducted (IGIDR) on Employment Guarantee for rural India against the background of the proposed enactment of an employment guarantee act by the government of India. The purpose was to discuss in an interactive manner various issues relating to the employment guarantee programme. There was an overall agreement in need

of such programme and on its feasibility in the current Indian context, this note is based on the deliberation at the round table but goes a bit beyond the discussions.

(9) Employment as a Right, says that, employment programme targeted at the poor is generally identified with poverty alleviation. The proposed act goes beyond poverty alleviation and recognizes employment as a universal legal right.

(10) Lionel Messias, 2003, says that, as each government department has different check measurements books, greedy officials gave contractors a free hand supporters of the ruling Telugu Desam Party and self-help group leaders were awarded most of the works on a nomination basis and not under recognized criteria worse. The Food Corporation of India released the free rice quota allotted by the centre as usual to the district administration from where it went to respective departments. As a result, the rice also travelled through the hands of corrupt contractors to rice millers, in turn was sold back to the FCI often unwittingly in the course of its business bought diverted FFWP rice from the millers as heavy rice and sold it to the fair price shops. Thus, the FFWP rice was strangely cycled and recycled with the connivance at millers' FCI officials and fair price shop dealers as well.

(11) Rice 'For Food For Work' business line, 17-3-2005, describes that, the centre has sanctioned, 1,25,413 million tones of rice to implement FFWP in eight districts of Andhra Pradesh during 2004-2005, the programme was launched in November, 2004. In 150 districts of the country Sampoorna Grameena Rozgar Yojana, Andhra Pradesh was sanctioned 4,02,000 million tones food grains during the same financial year, an official release said.

(12) Lakshminarayana, 2004, said that, as per the policy makers in New Delhi and in the respective states to incorporate of local political conditions into their plans for policy implementation. Caste discrimination neo-feudal interdependencies between poor tenants and their rich landlords and even criminal elements that dominate specific parts of the rural economy are factors that need to be carefully examined before committing resources to any district even the poorest ones. Otherwise there is a looking threat of misappropriation and wastage of scarce food resources in an already predominately food-insecure context.

(13) Barret C.B. Holden, and S.Clay, 2003, suggests that, although community level targeting can lead to some errors of inclusion due to political patronage. The greater effect is improved targeting to the poor by taking advantage of local knowledge of households needs and capabilities that is difficult to capture in measurable indicators such community targeting can help reducing targeting errors that result from exclusive reliance on self-targeting in areas where factor market imperfections break down the theorized positive relationship between household income or wealth and reservation FFWP participation wage.

(14) Ashok Mitra, 1980, says that, FFWP carries the possibility of being one of the best and most universally beneficial nutrition delivery programmes at very low cost with very high benefit leaving behind permanent residues provided. The food points are further fortified and the loopholes plugged, while the organizational and strengthened with community support. The programme has the additional possibility, become in powerful instrument of livelihood in the rural areas.

(15) Prabhu Nath Singh, 1975, says that, rural development has been designed to improve the

economic and social life of a specific group of people the rural poor invalids extending the benefits of development to the poorest among those who seek a livelihood in the rural areas.

(16) Kalipadu Basu, 1979, mentioned that, the persons without employment in India number about 25 million—about 12 per cent of the total labour forces of the country. The percentage is much higher as compared to that of other countries. For instance in the U.S.A. the ration of unemployment to total labour force is 5.2 per cent, in U.K. 3.3 per cent and in Japan it is 1.3 per cent only such a high unemployment nations a significant indication of the magnitude of the problem which warrants immediate attention as it will eat the very vitals of a country's economy through social conflicts, poverty, diseases and low productivity.

(17) Planning Commission,1974-1979, describes chronic unemployment, it says, is of course a very small part of the Indian unemployment problems because very few workers remain unemployed throughout the year. Millions of them find some work for some weeks or months and are forced into idleness in the rest of the year.

(18) Subratha Benerjee, 1979, argued that, the planning commission as millions of workers might not be able to get regular work even for a whole week. Ultimately measurement of unemployed days rather than unemployed 1973 that the persons were considered most realistic approach on that basis it was found for 1973 that the person day unemployed was 130 million days per week which was equivalent to 187.6 million person. In 1978 was estimated at 20.6 million persons year 16.5 million in the rural areas and 4.1 million in the urban areas.

(19) DP. Nayar, 1979, said that, the explanation of all these paradoxes lies in fact that in a labour surplus and capital scare economy like India adherence to capital intensive technique will further aggravate the problem of unemployment. Harrison rightly states that, unlike the developed regions of the world developing countries will not be able to solve their unemployment problems through the modern sector of the economics, even if these achieve rate of growth which are twice those are development countries.

(20) Edward J.Clay, explained that, rural public works and Food For Work Programme. Thus he says that the belief and rehabilitation case histories reveal the severe tension between immediate employment creation and income generation objectives and the longer-term concerns to create socially valuable assets and to avoid beneficiary dependency.

(21) N.P. Singh, 1980, says that, the Bangladesh study concludes that the quality of work performed closely reflects this: The importance of motivation is underlined by contrasting reports and poor work and behaviour in Ethiopia in reforestation projects in the early 1970s before land reform and the high standards of construction in soil conservation and rehabilitation projects a decade later.

(22) Ashok Mitra, 1980, informed that, FFWP carries the possibility of being one of the best and the most universally beneficial nutrition level. The FFWP carries nutrition deliver at very low cost with very high benefit, leaving behind permanent residues provided the food points and further fortified and the loopholes plugged. While the organizational and delivered systems are progressively improved and strengthened with community support. The programme has the additional possibility of becoming a powerful instrument of desirable social change.

(23) A. Ethirajulu Naidu, 1990, said that, Poverty alleviation through NREP a study, describes that Chittoor district in Andhra Pradesh is a backward district as is one among the district reserved for scheduled castes. Unemployment and underemployment pose a problem in rural areas. This gets accentuated during the lean period of Agriculture operations and raising the income level of the poor and strengthening the rural infrastructure.

(24) Naveeen Chandra Koshi, 1978, says that, the Sixth Plan has made an advance in right direction by emphasizing schemes like FFWP. Anthyodoya, revised minimum needs programme and so on, which are expected to make a dent on rural unemployment problem.

(25) Kummuidini Dandekar and Manju Sathe, 1980, advocated the planning department of the state regarding the needed employment for the weaker sections, which included landless labourers and the lower most 10 per cent cultivators in rural Maharashtra State. These were based on the findings of the 25th round of NSS conducted in 1970-71. The estimated unemployed mandays were 14 crores as wage bill for EGS.

(26) R.Thukral, 1980, describes, how the FFWP is being administered at three levels in the states. It coordinated by the ministry of rural reconstruction at the central level. It was noted during the course of the list to various projects and in discussions with the officials of the state government. The main driving force behind implementation of the programme was the commitment of the official incharge of the community.

(27) D.P. Gupta, 1978, views, the FFWP was conceived and undertaken with the twin objectives of creating

avenue of employment, on the one hand, constructing valuable durable assets for the welfare of the community.

(28) Ved. Basin 1979, says that, the FFWP is an inadequate durable community assets unemployment and underemployment are well associated with the rural scene. In the state Janata Government initiation of the FFWP, which aims at providing employment opportunities throughout the length and breadth of this sprawling state. The extension of the programme in the next few years will indeed provide a fresh fillip to this mass movement of creation community assets for the masses themselves who are involved in it.

(29) Shrimati Indira Gandhi, 1982, FFWP final evaluation yojana 16-31, May 1982 describes, our national motto is "satyame vajayate—Truth alone wins in our daily lives" dedication to truth and toil the bedrock of respect progress and prosperity. In one state foodgrains were utilised for the purchase of cooking-gas and furniture and keep up of the government building. Government converted grain into cash meeting cost of construction school buildings, dispensaries, and panchayat house.

(30) S.C. Varma, 1981, said that, the FFWP, the present on-going programme, came into being because large stocks of food grains were available in 1977. The disposal of stocks was causing some concern and in the context, it was decided that a large sized works programme should be launched in the rural areas subject to the condition that the wages be paid in kind and not in cash.

(31) The programme rural India, 1979, says that, FFWP has four objectives. To generate more employment opportunities for the rural poor. The build up durable

rural community assets such as roads and irrigation projects. To help maintain village public works, to utilise surplus food grain stocks for productive efforts. FFWP aims at maintenance of these rural assets and creation of new ones, on the one hand, and providing employment to the needy poor on the other.

(32) Venugopal, 2004, explained that, the ministry of rural development guidelines make interesting reading section 3.4 says payment of wages shall be made on fixed day in a week preferably a day before the local market day. It would appear that the food paid out to workers would be bartered at the weekly market in the bartering process the poor quality grain the workers earn in variably under valued the commodities he buys over valued.

(33) Krishna Ananth, says that, the FFWP is being implemented rural area. The government distribution wages under the FFWP kind cash and food grains. Quantity of 31.5 lakh tonnes of rice, worth about Rs. 3150 crore, given free of cost by the government of India, and cash of Rs. 990 crore. Against 7 lakh works sanctioned Rs. 12,5,83 lakh works were completed, creating 28.40 crore mandays and distributing 26.34 lakh tones of rice to the workers.

(34) Chandra Banprasad, 2005, advocated that, as per guidelines issued by the government. The workers under the FFWP can choose payment of wages per manday in any of the three options: 5 kgs of rice plus Rs. 30 or 8 kgs of rice plus Rs.10 or 10 kgs of rice without any cash component. The selection of works under the FFWP and release of rice was done in discriminatory and not on the basis of the severity of drought situation.

(35) B.R. Sreeramulu, said that, according to the Hindu newspaper article in Cuddapah District in Andhra

Pradesh Subharaju was illegally transporting FFWP rice MRO Lakshmaiah Circle Inspector. The Chinnachowk police seized 35 bags of food for work rice, which was loaded at fair shops in Sankarapuram in Cuddapah town on Sunday.

(36) According to these articles the state secretary Sudhakar Reddy demanded at the mandal level to allot works relating to FFWP and to supervise its implementation. The alleged that the state government had miserably failed to provide relief although 912 mandals in state had been provided with relief under the impact of drought. The CPI functionary demanded work for the poor and the helpless under the FFWP and asserted that there should be no place for contractors and middlemen. He regretted that although six crore tones of food grains were available with FCI godowns.

(37) Sandeep Bagchi, 1987, said that, the International Labour Organisation conducted a survey of the implementation of NREP in the states of Gujarat and Karnataka in the year 1984. It was observed that on sample projects the average employment provided labourer was 51 days in Gujarat and 55 days in Karnataka the survey revealed that the programme was found to more effective in providing in long term and continuous employment for the unemployed and underemployed.

(38) Das, says that, the JRY has not been very successful the income gained through wages under JRY too small an amount to help the poor, the cross the poverty line. The production assets created through the programme hardly reflected the priorities of the local people.

(39) Lakshmaiah made a study, in Chittoor District of Andhra Pradesh to assess the impact of the NREP on income and extent of gainful employment of

sample beneficiaries one of the major findings of the study was that progress of the programme was satisfactory, in the sense that, all utilization of funds and creation of additional employment were achieved. The analysis revealed that the target group landless labour and the category of scheduled castes derived minimum advantage from NREP, in term of earning additional income and getting additional mandays of employment.

Chapterisation

The thesis is presented in six chapters. The First chapter deals with Introduction to the research study.

The Second chapter focuses on the beneficiaries of these programmes, District profile and selected mandals, distribution of food grains under Food For Work Programme.

The Third chapter is about Distribution of wages under the Food For Work Programme.

Operationalisation and Problems of Food For Work Programme is dealt in the Fourth chapter.

The Fifth chapter discusses the Monitoring and Evaluation of the Food For Work Programme.

Chapter Six gives the Summary and Conclusion.

Profile of Chittoor District

The impact of any programme can be assessed only with a thorough understanding of the profile of the study area. Keeping this in view, an attempt is made in this chapter to present profile of the study area *i.e.,* Chittoor District in the drought prone Rayalaseema Region of the state of Andhra Pradesh.

Area

The total area of district is 15,152 sq kms comprising 1,540 villages of which, 1,489 are inhabited. The district comprises three revenue divisions viz. Chittoor, Tirupati and Madanapalli and these divisions divided into 66 revenue mandals.

The district derives rainfall mostly from the south-west and North East monsoons and the average annual rainfall is the incidence of the rainfall is not uniform and therefore, the district is frequently prone to drought condition. The upland region of the district comprising erstwhile taluks of Palamaner, Kuppam, Punganur, Madanapalli and

Vayalapadu derives major share of rainfall from the south west monsoons, while the eastern part of district gets the maximum benefit from the North East monsoon.

Chittoor district is one of the four districts in Rayalaseema region of Andhra Pradesh. Chittoor district was constituted on 1st April, 1911, comprison Taluks of Chittoor, Palamaneru and Chandragiri transferred from north Arcot district of Tamil Nadu, Mandanpalle and Vayalpadu Taluks from Kadapa districts and Ex Zamindari areas of Punganur, Srikalahasti, Puttur and old Karvetinagaram Estate by 1-12-1928 Kangundhi Taluk of North Arcot district with the exception of 22 villages was transferred to Palamaner Taluk and in 1950 under the province and states Absorption of enclaves order, 8 villages of Mysore state were transferred to Palamaneru Taluk. The next major change in jurisdiction of the district took place on 1st April 1960 as a result Pataskar Award. Consequent on the re-organisation of the state on linguistic basis a major portion of Taluk was transferred to Chengalpattu district of Tamil Nadu. Instead one Taluk known as Sathyavedu comprising 76 villages of Puttur Taluk, 19 villages of Tiruthani Taluk was constituted and added to Chittoor district. Also from the same date, the sub Taluks of Kuppam and Bangarupalem were constituted transferring 220 villages from Palamaneru Taluk and 3 villages from Krishnagiri Taluk of Salem district of Tamil Nadu to form Kuppam sub-taluk and 145 villages from Chittoor Taluk to form Bangarupalem sub-taluk, subsequently Kuppam and Bangarupalem were made full fledged taluks.

The above 11 taluks of the district were re-organised into 15 taluks and 20 Panchayath samithis again the above 15 taluks of the district G.O.Ms. No. 569 Revenue (Mandal-2) Dept. Dt. 22-05-1985 subsequently 65 Mandal Praja Parishads were formed.

Topography

The Chittoor district is bound by on the North by Anantapur and Kadapa district, on the East by Nellore district and

Chengalpattu district of Tamil Nadu and Karnataka States. The districts cover an extent of 15-152 kms. It is divided into 3 Revenue divisions' *viz.*, Chittoor, Tirupati and Madanapalli. It is situated between "120°-37" to "140°-8" of North latitude and 780°-33″ to 790°-55″ of the Eastern longitude.

The District can be divided into Two Natural Divisions

The mountainous plateau on the west comprising the 31 mandals of Madanapalli division.

The plains on the East are comprising the mandals of Puttur. Narayanavanam, Vadamalpet, Kammapalli, Karvetinagar, Vedurukuppam, S.R. Puram, Palasamudram, Nagari, Nindra, Vijayapuram, Pichattur, Nagalapuiram, Sathyavedu, Varadayapallem. B.N. Kandriga, Kovanurv, Thattambedu, Srikalahasti and Yerpedu.

The mandal viz, Chittoor, G.D.Nellore, Puthalapattu, Penumuru, Gudipala, Yadamari, Thavbanampalli and Irala stand almost as dividing line. The Eastern Ghats are predominant in the western region and they gradually bend towards the sacred hills of Tirupati. Passing through Chandragiri erst while Taluk and entering Nellore District. The general elevation of the mountainous part of the district is 2500 ft., above sea level.

Climate

The climate of the district is dry and healthy. The upland's subdivision 31 mandals in Madanapalli division are comparatively cooler than the eastern ones except Chittoor where the climate is moderate.

Rainfall

The district has the benefit of receiving rainfall during both south-west and north-east monsoon periods, while the normal rainfall of the district for the south-west monsoon period is 438.00 mm while that of North East monsoon period is 396.00 mm.

The rainfall received during the winter period and hot weather period is negligible. Their respective normal being 12.0 mm and 88.0 mm. The annual normal rainfall of the district is 934.0 mm.

Table 2.1 : Rainfall

Sl.No.	Source	Rainfal
1.	South Western monsoon	450.3
2	North East monsoon	753.4
3.	Winter period	00.2
4.	Hot weather period	1319.7
	Total	**2523.6**

Source: Handbook of Statistics 2005-2006.Chief Planning Officer, Chittoor, p. 25.

Rivers

The rivers flowing in the district are non-perennial in nature in that they remain dry for a major apart of the year. Of these rivers, river Ponnai which is tributary of river Palar rises in erstwhile Chittoor taluk and flowing towards the south, joins the Palar in Tamil Nadu. The Swarnamukhi another important river which rises in the eastern ghats in erst-while Chandragiri Taluk has its course through out the mandals of erstwhile Chandragiri Taluk and part of erst-while Srikalahasthi Taluk and ultimately flows in the Nellore district other such important rivers of the district are the Kusastali, the Bheema, the Pincha, the Kalyani, the Araniyar and the Pedderu which flow in different mandals of the district, besides the above rivers, there are a number of small hilly streams flowing in the district.

Soils

The major portion of the district is covered with red soils with portions of alluvial soil in Chittoor and Bangarupalem erst-while Taluks. According to an assessment made on the basis of village records, 57 per cent of the soils of the district are red loamy and 34 per cent red sandy the remaining 9 per cent is covered by black clay (3 per cent) black loamy (2 per cent) black sandy (1 per cent) and red clay (3 per cent).

Minerals

The district is not rich in mineral wealth; steatite is the only mineral mine in Puttur and G.D.Nellore erstwhile block areas of the district. However, the occurrence of gold, iron and red moulding sand are also noticed in certain parts of the district. In Bisanatham area of Kuppam erstwhile Taluk, the Auriferour veoms are 22 per cent wide and carry an average gold content of 5.190-wts of gold per tonne. Iron ore occurred in intimate association with in Voyalpadu, Srikalahasti and Puttur erst-while Taluks.

Irrigation

There are 8 medium irrigation projects in the district. They are Swarnamukhi Anicut, Aranjiyar, Mallimadugu, and Kalingi, Bahuda, Siddalagandi, Krishanapuram Reservoir and Pedderu project. The total registered ayacut under the eight projects is 15,310 hectares. There are 7512 minor irrigation tanks with a total ayacut of 54, 336/14 Hectares. The district occupies a pride of place in the number of irrigation wells totalling 1,16,239.

Population

According to census of 2001, it is reported that the district has a total population of 37,45,875 of which 18,89,690 are males 50.45 per cent and females are 18,56,185 49.55 per cent, as per the 2001 census, the rural population in Chittoor. Urban population of the district is (8,11,030) 21.70 per cent.

Density of Population

The density of population in the district was as per 2001 census is 247. The density of population of the Chittoor district is not much higher than that of the state average 277 of the Andhra Pradesh.

Political Profile

The Congress party is the dominant party in the district the second place goes to Telugu Desam party. The presence of the left parties is not visible. These parties are dominated by the Reddy community caste of the district. Another emerging castes are Kamma and Balija who are rivals to the Reddy community in the field of politics. The other castes of the district are Mala, Madiga, Yanadi, and Yerukala, belonging to the deprived classes.

Scheduled Caste and Scheduled Tribes

According to 2001 census, 7,02,320 people have been recorded as belonging to the scheduled caste. The per cent of the S.C. population in the district is 18.75 to total population in the district is slighty higher than the state average of 16.19 per cent during the 2001 census. The main communities that comprise the SC population are Mala, Madiga, Adi-Andhra and Adi-Dravida.

According to the 2001 census, the total population of Scheduled Tribes is 1,28,085. The per cent of scheduled Tribes in the district is 3.42. The main tribes in the district are Yerukula and Yanadis and a fewer number are Sugali.

According to 2001 census in the Chittoor district, 65 per cent are pucca houses, 35 per cent are katcha houses. There is availability of household amenities like electricity, safe drinking water, and toilet facilities in Chittoor district as per the 2001 census. Majority of households in rural areas 95 per cent has facilities, drinking water and 35 per cent have toilet facilities. But these three facilities are available to 99 per cent of the urban households of the district. This shows that majority of rural households, lack of the amenities when compared to the urban households this indicates rural households still suffer from lack of basic amenities.

Demographic Profile of Chittoor District

As per 2001 census, the total population of the district is 37,45,875 this is 6.30 per cent of the States' population. The density of population in the district is 18,247 per sq. km.

Table 2.2 : Population of Chittoor District 1901-2001

Sl.No	Year	Population	Variation	
			No. of persons	Per cent
1.	1901	1124261	—	—
2.	1911	1177489	53228	4.73
3.	1921	1209752	32263	2.74
4.	1931	1331517	121765	10.07
5.	1941	1497778	166261	12.49
6.	1951	1666741	168963	11.28
7.	1961	1915331	248590	14.91
8.	1971	2285536	370205	19.33
9.	1981	1737316	451780	19.77
10.	1991	3261118	523802	19.14
11.	2001	3745875	484757	14.86

Source: Hand Book of Statistics 2005-2006, Chief Planning Officer, Chittoor.P.1.

Above Table 2.2 shows that, the Trends in population growth in Chittoor district during 1991 to 2001.The population in Chittoor district has been increasing steadily since 1901. In 1901, the total population of the district was 11,24,261 and it has increased to 1,17,71,489 registering an increase of 4.73 per cent. The total population of the district has increased by 2.49 per cent between 1921 to 1931 and between 1931 to 1941 respectively. The rate of increase in population of the district and the increase is more marked. Male and female population in Chittoor district after 1951.

Table 2.3 : Male and Female Population in Chittoor District

Sl. No.	Year	Males	Females	Total (in lakhs)
1.	1991	16.58 (50.84)	16.03 (49.16)	32.61 (100)
2.	2001	18.90	18.56	37.46 (100)

Source: Hand Book of Statistics 2005-2006, Chief Planning Officer, Chittoor.

It is evident that through the per cent of increase in total population according to 2001 census i.e., 37.46 per cent has increased as compared to the percentage of population according to 1991 census i.e., 32.61 per cent of increase in the population of male and female has not registered any significant increase.

Table 2.4 : Size of Rural and Urban Population in Chittoor District

S.No	Year	Rural	Urban	Total
1.	1991	26.15 (80.19)	6.46 (19.81)	32.61 (100)
2.	2001	29.35	8.11	37.46

Source: Hand Book of Statistics 2005-2006, Chief Planning Officer, Chittoor.

Above Table 2.4 Reveals that the rural population in the total population of the district decreased to per cent in 2001, from 80.19 per cent in 1991.

Table 2.5 : Shows Distribution of Population by Caste Wise in Chittoor District

Sl.No.	Year	S.C.P	Pecentage to Total	S.T. Population	P. To.T
1	1991	5.99	18.37	1.05	3.22
2	2001	7.02	18.68	1.28	3.41

Source: Hand Book of Statistics 2005-2006, Chief Planning Officer, Chittoor.

Above Table 2.5 shows that the working status of the population in the district according to 1991 and 2001 census respectively distribution of population according to working status in Chittoor district.

Table 2.6

Sl. No.	Year	Main workers	Marginal workers	Non workers	Cultivators	Agricultural labourers
1.	1991	14.02 (42.99)	0.96 (2.94)	17.63 (54.06)	5.29 (16.22)	4.90 (15.02)
2.	2001	14.63	2.90	19.93	5.28	6.30

Source: Hand Book of Statistics 2005-2006, Chief Planning Officer Chittoor.

Above Table 2.6 reveals that, the per cent of non-workers marginal workers and the cultivators according to 2001 census, as compared to the 1991 census. It is however noticed that the per cent of agriculture labourers and main workers registered an increase in the total population in 2001 as compared with that of 1991.

Agro Economic Profile

Land Utilisation

Reveals the land utilisation pattern in the district Forests cover 30.11 per cent of the total geographical area in the District during 1993-1994. The net area sown accounts for 32.88 per cent and land put to non-agricultural uses for 9.38 per cent.

Table 2.7 : Land Utilisation in Chittoor District during 2002-2006

Sl.No.	Category	2005-06	2005-04	2004-03	2003-02
1	2	3	4	5	6
1.	Forests	451345	451345	451345	451345
2.	Barren uncultivable land	164000	164220	164265	164267
3.	Land put to non-agricultural uses	142334	142254	142254	142253

1	2	3	4	5	6
4.	Cultivatable waste	42458	43537	39512	39529
5.	Per cent pastures and other Grazing lands	36291	36502	36527	36527
6.	Land under miscellaneous tree crops and groves not included net area sown	25092	250165	25173	25197
7.	Current fallows	105898	114254	161759	186969
8.	Other fallows land	116301	117707	126276	128447
9.	Net area sown	415043	403774	351674	324243
10.	Total geographical area	1498778	149878	1498778	1498778
11.	Total cropped area	457548	443005	390336	362771
12.	Area sown more than once	42505	39229	36293	38528

Source: Hand Book Statistics 2005-2006, Chief Planning Officer Chittoor.

Cropping Pattern

The cropping pattern depends on several factors such as the availability of irrigation facilities, Soil conditions etc., in Chittoor district, cropping pattern is influenced mostly by rainfall. Groundnut and paddy are the major crops growth in the district Ragi, and sugarcane are the other important crops raised in the district.

Groundnut occupies the largest area, accounting for 49.8 per cent of the gross cropped area and it is mostly raised as a rain-fed crop. Next in order, the area under paddy accounts for 1.33 per cent of the gross cropped area sugarcane, 1.24 Ragi 2.63, Jower occupy 0.47 of the total cropped area respectively the area covered under chillies is only 0.66 per cent. Under fruits and vegetables it is 6.78 per cent and under total cereals and millet 25.33 per cent obviously groundut and paddy are the principal crops in the district.

Table 2.8 : Area under the Principal Crops in Chittoor District 2005-2006

Sl. No.	Crop	Area in acres	Per cent to total (areas in Ha)
1.	Groundnut	195337	49.8
2.	Paddy	5207	1.33
3.	Sugarcane	4877	1.24
4.	Ragi	10,296	2.63
5.	Barra	1918	0.48
6.	Jowar	1858	0.47
7.	Chillies	2618	0.66
8.	Total areas and mullets	99270	25.35
9.	Fruits and vegetable	70099	17.90
	Total	**391,48**	**100**

Source: Hand Book of Statistics 2005-2006, Chief Planning Officer Chittoor pp.42-49.

High Yielding Varieties Programme

Agriculture has assumed greater importance in the district with the adoption of improved agriculture practices such as the use of high yielding variety seeds of paddy, Jowar, groundnut, mechanization of agriculture and increase use of chemical fertilizers. The high yielding varieties especially in respect of paddy and Jowar have spread rapidly and made their impact in terms of increase in production and productivity.

The high yielding varieties are introduced in the district for the first time during 1967-68, since then the area under high yielding varieties has increased steadily.

Agriculture Machines and Implements

New technology envisages the use of improved implements and machinery. The number of various items of agriculture machinery and implements used in Chittoor district 2005-2006 are given.

Table 2.9 : Agricultural Machinery and Implements used in Chittoor District

Sl. No.	Item	Number
1.	Total plough-shares	256617
2.	Water pumps for irrigation purpose	112020
3.	Tractors	4118
4.	Sugarcane crushers	9522
5.	Sprayers & Dusters	3257
6.	Bullock-carts	2295

Source: Hand Book of Statistics 2005-2006, Chief Planning Officer, Chittoor, pp. 56-57.

Livestock and Poultry

There is good potential for the development of animal husbandry as a subsidiary occupation in view of large number of small and marginal farmers in the district. Among the various allied activities, dairy farming, poultry farming sheep rearing and calf rearing are being promoted. The livestock not only provide subsidiary sources of income to agriculturists, but also accounts for a significant portion of the trade in the district. The district has the largest number of cattle and poultry birds among the districts of the Rayalaseema Region. Milch animal provide the secondary source of income to the agriculture families in the district. There is one dairy unit and more than 1.5 lakh liters of milk per day is marketed. Milk is procured through 717 village level milk 10 co-operatives societies in the district. There are milk-chilling center at Madanapalli, Pitchatur, V. Kota, Piler and Srikalahasti. Thus, live stock and milch animals are one of the major sources of income to the households in the district.

Table 2.10 : Livestock and Poultry Population in Chittoor District 2005-2006

Sl.No.	Category	Total	Per cent to total
1.	Cattle (a) Male (b) Female (c) Young stock	8,36,334	8.20
2.	Buffaloes	1,39,498	1.36
3.	Sheep	9,37,668	9.19
4.	Goats	2,45,855	2.41
5.	Donkeys	358	0.00351
6.	Pigs	11,398	0.11
7.	Poultry	80,23,378	78.68
8.	Ducks	2129	0.04
9.	Others	361	0.0035
	Total	**1,01,96,979**	**100**

Source: Hand Book of Statistics 2005-2006, Chief Planning Officer Chittoo, pp. 72-74.

Fisheries

The district has 266 tanks with total water spread area of 16.879 hectares. The fish catch from these sources is around 20 thousand metric tonnes "Fish culture marketing scheme" is taken up this year to supply inputs for fish rearing and provides assistance to fisherman's co-operative societies in the district through fish farmers development Agency.

Sericulture

Sericulture has been making rapid strides of progress in the district because of favourable agro-climatic conditions. As of now 42,700 acres are under mulberry cultivation in the district about 42,030 sericulture are engaged in mulberry rearing 20,200 small, 15,420 marginal and 7,311 big farmers, have undertaken the activity. Mostly small and marginal farmers have undertaken this enterprise in Madanapalli and Chittoor revenue divisions in the districts. Necessary infrastructural facilities such as gram seed farms, silk reeling unit and market centers are being set up in the district under various schemes. There are at present 8 granges in the government sector and 1 private grange at Palamaner, 5 seed farms, 9 silk reeling units and 3 market centers at Madanapalli, Palamaner and Kuppam are also functioning. Besides this higher capacity grange of 50 lakhs laying is established recently which was not producing to full capacity with all these facilities more and more farmers especially in the district which is frequently prone to drought conditions, however, the reeling of silk is yet to become popular in the district and efforts are on to train entrepreneurs.

Horticulture

The district with tremendous potential for horticulture development is third in the state in terms of the land already brought under horticulture plantation. At present, mango orchards are raised in 53, 461 acres with a yield of 2.14 lakhs mango. Cashew crop raised in 673 acres, within annual yield of 1,615 tonnes. There is an organised market of mangoes fruit export from this district. In addition 30 pulping industries are functioning in the district to absorb considerable mango production farmers. These are opting for the conversion of agricultural land for better remuneration.

Irrigation

There are eight medium irrigation projects in the districts. Swarnamukhi, Aanicut, Araniyar, Mallimadugu, Kalangh, Bahuda, Siddalangandi project, Krishnapuram Reservoir and Pedderu project.

The total registered area under the eight projects in 41,429 acres. However, there are 8,241 minor irrigation sources with a total ayacut of 1,57,990 acres. The district occupies a pride of place in the number of irrigation wells totalling to 1,28,364 in number.

The distribution of net irrigated area by different sources in Chittoor district.

Table 2.11 : Area Irrigated by Different Sources in Chittoor District during 2005-2006

Sl.No.	Source of Irrigation	Total	Per cent
1.	Canals	1702	1.07
2.	Tanks	45736	28.81
3.	Wells	35,800	22.55
4.	Tube wells	75416	47.51
5.	Other sources	73	0.04
	Total	**158727**	**100**

Source: Hand Book of Statistics 2005-2006, Chief Planning Officer, Chittoor, pp. 64.

Data pertaining to 2005-2006 reveal that wells, as a source of irrigation constitute 22.55 per cent followed by tanks (i.e 8.81) evidently wells constitute a major source of irrigation in the District. In 2005-06 the area irrigated acres, with canals accounted for 1.07. tanks for 28.81 tube wells for 47.51 and wells for 22.55 per cent.

Table 2.12: Gross Area Irrigated during 2005-06

Sl.No.	Category	Area in Hec.	(In acres) Per cent
1.	Net area irrigated	1578806	80.17
2.	Area irrigated more than once	39264	19.82
	Gross Area Irrigated Total	**198270**	**100**

Source: Hand Book of Statistics 2005-2006, Chief Planning Officer Chittoor pp.64.

Socio-economic Infrastructure Profile

Education: The district has 4,492 primary schools, 1021 upper primary schools, 789 High schools. Schools for physically challenge other special school 7, there were 131, junior colleges, 56-degree colleges, colleges for professional and special education. Private, and Government 40 during the year 2005-06. Four universities are situated at Tirupati. There are 3 polytechnic institutes and 4 individuals training institutes besides one medical, one veternary science college, one agriculture college and one engineering college in Kuppam one medical college, Engineering college. The Teacher Training institute at Karvetinagaram and S.V. School for deaf and dumb at Tirupati are functioning in the district.

Power

The district totally electified. During the year 2005-2006 to share of agriculture in the total consumption of electricity was 7,93,796 and kilowatts and for domestic purposes it was 3,44,377 KW.

Communication

The district has a fairly satisfactory system and network of communication. At the end of 2005-2006 there were 872 post offices, 62 telegraph offices, 181 telephone exchanges, 142316 telephone connections, 11781 public call offices.

Transport

The district is well connected by means of rail and road with all important commercial centers by a net work of roads and some even by railways, Renigunta and Pakala two Railway Junctions in the district.

Industries

The Chittoor district is one of the backward districts in the country in the absence of mineral wealth in the district. There is scope only for development of agro-based industries like fruit processing units, oil extracting units and silk reeling industries. Since the district happens to be in the backward area government is offering incentives of the entrepreneurs for setting up on industries in the district.

There are two well functioning industrial estates in Chittoor and Tirupati and the district has 61 large and medium scale industries with total strength of employees of 12,884 and 4,113. Small scale and village & cottage industries with total employees of 26,857. The Kuppam belt in the district is having a number of granite polishing industries, which are thriving well. Srikalahasti has a unique feature of having a number of kalankar art units, Puttur, Nagari, Ekambarakuppam are famous for cloth products and substantial quantity is being expected to various western countries.

The state government has launched an extensive campaign of industrial development in the district by taking up a variety of schemes. They include self-employment schemes incentive campaign for setting up of electronic estates, craft gold, and raw material depots, industrial. Co-operatives, marketing societies and offering subsidies, incentives such as interest subsidy power tariff concessions etc.

Services

The district has 18 government hospitals 3 private hospitals 3 primary health centers, dispnesaries besides there are 35 ayurvedic 15 and 29-homeopathy dispensaries.one super speciality hospital is at Tirupati.

Banking

There are 26 branch offices of various commercial banks by end of 2005-2006 various bank branches have gone up to 245 of which 149 are the branch offices commercial banks, 71 are branch offices of R.R.Bs and 22 cooperative banks.

The average population served by Bank branch at the end of March 1992 was estimated at 11,311.

The important institutional offices of various commercial banks the district agriculture development bank, the state industrial development corporation and a number of co-operatives are functioning at various level in addition to these there are also a number of special developmental agencies and programmes catering to a variety of special needs and problems in the district like 1) Chittoor district Harijana and Girijana Development Corporation. 2) A.P. Scheduled Castes co-operative financial corporation. 3) A.P.Backward classes co-operative finance corporation etc.

Profile of Puthalapattu Mandal—the Study Area

Puthalapattu is one of the 66 revenue mandals in the Chittoor district; it has geographical area of 156.60 sq. kms it is bound on the East by Penumuru on the west by Irala on the North by Pakala and South by Chittoor. Puthalapattu mandal comprises 21 villages and 245 hamlets. According to 1991 census, the total population was 44,676 of which there were 22,458 males and 22,218 females. It is multi-caste mandal. Scheduled Castes total population is 11190, males 5654, females 5536, Scheduled Tribes total population 996, males 514, and females 484. The entire populations in the mandal live in villages. Density of population is 285.

There are 8142 cultivators and 9251 agriculture laboures of the land use in the mandal, forest cover 16 per cent, barren and uncultivable land 8 per cent land put to non-agriculture use 11 per cent permanent pastures and other grazing lands 2 per cent cultivable waste 6 per cent, and other fallow lands 4 per cent. Net area sown is 31 per cent.

There are sources of major irrigation in the mandal. The irrigated area covered under tanks in Rabi season is 190 acres. Area covered under tube wells in Kharif is 522 acres and in Rabi is 440 acres, other wells covered in Kharif is 139 acres and Rabi it is 23 acres, net area irrigated in Kharif is 592 acres and in Rabi it is 190 acres.

Total cattle population live stock in the mandal is 13200 of which there are 446 buffaloes 9815 sheep, 2866 goats 0 horses, 325 pigs and the live stock population in the mandal is 26672 poultry birds number 163127.

The literates constitute 68.94 per cent of which 80.72 per cent were males and 45,708 per cent females in the total population. There are 78 primary schools, 10 upper primary schools, 11 high schools and one Govt. Junior College and one degree college in the mandal.

Agriculture is the major source of occupation in the mandal. All the villages are electrified in the mandal out of 269 hamlets 267 are electrified. There are 4826 agriculture services and 259 industrial services.

There is one scheduled nationalized bank and one rural bank mandal provide crop loans and term loans to weaker sections. There is sub post office with 11 branches offices located at various places at the mandal.

Profile of Pakala Mandal—The Study Area

Pakala is one of the 66 revenue mandals in the Chittoor district. It has geographical area of 125.49 sq. kms. Chandragiri bound it on the east on the west by Irala on the north by Pulicherla and south by Puthalapattu mandal; Pakala mandal comprises 15 villages and 238 hamlets according to 1991 censers. The total population was 51,92; there were 28,414 males and 28,388 female. It is multi-caste mandal. Scheduled caste constitutes 12,712 and scheduled tribes 1,172 of the total population the entire population in the mandal line in village. Density of population is 453.

There are 8,470 cultivators and 90, 36 agriculture labourers of the land use in the mandal. Forest cover 18 per cent. Land put to non-agriculture use 2 per cent. Permanent pasture and other grazing land 4 per cent. Cultivable waste 7 per cent and other fallow lands 10 per cent, net area sown 35 per cent.

There are sources of major irrigation in the mandal. The irrigated area covered under tanks in Kharif season is155 acres. Area covered under tube wells in Kharif is 366 acres and in Rabi in 242 acres, other wells covered in Kharif is 820 acres and Rabi it is 537 acres, net area irrigated in Kharif is 1255 acres and in Rabi it is 655 acres.

Total cattle population in the mandal is 16,699 of which, there are 458 buffaloes 5,671 sheep 4,230 goats, 0 horses 41 pigs and the live stock population in the mandal is 115823 poultry birds number.

The literate constitute 72.20 per cent, of which 83.46 per cent were male and 60.90 per cent, females in the total population. There are 77 primary schools, 7 upper primary schools, 2 municipal high schools, private aid one, un-aided two schools and two junior college, one degree college in the mandal.

Agriculture is the staple occupation in the Pakala mandal. All the villages of the mandal is fully electrified in the mandal; out of hamlets 200 are 4016 agriculture services and 149 industrial services. There are five scheduled nationalized banks and one co-operative bank existed in the mandal, provide crop loan and term loan to the weaker section of the farmers. There are sub post offices with 19 branch offices located at various places in the mandal.

Progress of FFWP Study Area

Table 2.13 : Distribution of Sample Members according to Age Group

Sl.No.	Age group	Pakala Mandal	Percen-tage	Puthala-pattu mandal	Percen-tage	Total Member	Per cent
1	20-30	6	12.00	15	30.00	21	21.00
2	31-40	20	40.00	13	26.00	33	33.00
3	41-50	24	48.00	22	44.00	46	46.00
	Total	50	100.00	50	100.00	100.00	100.00

Source: Field Survey Data, FFWP.

Table 2.13 shows that the field survey age group between 20-30 in Pakala mandal 6 member, 12 per cent Puthalapattu mandal 15, member, per cent 30, total 21, comparing both Mandals Puthalapattu mandal is high per cent 30 per cent. Age group between 31-40 in Pakala mandal 20 members, 40 per cent between ages, in Puthalapattu mandal, totals members both mandal 33 members, total per cent 33. Age group between 41-50 above in Pakala mandal between is 24 members, per cent is 48, and Puthalapattu mandal 22 members, per cent is 44. Comparing both mandals Pakala mandal is high per cent both mandals 46 members.

Table 2.14 : Gender Distribution of beneficiaries of FFWP according to Sex

Sl.No.	Gender	Pakala Mandal	Percent	Puthala-pattu mandal	Percent	Total Member	Per cent
1.	Male	27	54.00	25	50.00	52	52.00
2.	Female	23	46.00	25	50.00	48	48.00
	Total	**50**	**100.00**	**50**	**100.00**	**100.00**	**100.00**

Source: Field Survey Data, FFWP.

Above Table 2.14 shows that gender wise population male and female members are working under FFWP. Two mandals in Pakala mandal is male 27 members, 54 per cent and female 23 members, 46 per cent. Puthalapattu mandal male 25 members, and females 25 members, both per cent 100. Both

Table 2.15 : Social Classification of Beneficiaries of FFWP

Sl.No.	Case	Pakala Mandal	Percent	Puthala-pattu mandal	Percent	Total Member	Per cent
1	OC	24	48.00	15	30.00	39	39.00
2	BC	12	24.00	9	18.00	21	21.00
3	SC	14	28.00	26	52.00	40	40.00
	Total	**50**	**100.00**	**50**	**100.00**	**100.00**	**100.00**

Source: Field survey, Data FFWP.

mandal total male are 52 members total of female 48 members. Comparing to male in Pakala mandal it is higher than to the number of male numbers Puthalapattu mandal. According to the total female members comparing with higher in Pakala mandal that of Puthalapattu mandal is higher than that of Pakala mandal.

Table 2.15 shows that, Pakala and Puthalapattu mandal OC, BC, SC categories are participants of FFWP. Pakala mandal OC, category 24 members, 48 per cent, BC category 12 members, 24 per cent SC category 14 members, 28 per cent. Puthalapattu mandal total OC category member's 15, per cent 30, BC category 9 members, per cent 18, SC category 26 members, per cent 26. Both mandals total OC category 39 members, BC category 21 members, SC category 40 members working under FFWP. Comparing both mandals in the Pakala mandal more OC, BC category people participate category in FFWP in Puthalapattu mandal are more than that of Pakala mandal.

Table 2.16 : Education Levels of the Beneficiaries of FFWP

Sl.No.	Education	Pakala Mandal	Percent	Puthala-pattu mandal	Percent	Total Member	Per cent
1	Illiterate	16	32.00	20	40.00	36.00	52.00
2	Literate	34	68.00	30	60.00	64.00	48.00
	Total	**50**	**100.00**	**50**	**100.00**	**100.00**	**100.00**

Source: Field Survey, Data FFWP.

Table 2.16 shows literate and illiterate people participants in FFWP in both mandal. Illiterates Pakala mandal are 16 member, 32 per cent, Puthalapattu mandal 20 member 40 per cent, total members 36, per cent 36. Literate people in Pakala mandal 34 members, 68 per cent, Puthalapattu mandal 30 members, 60 per cent total 64 members according to literate ratio. Pakala mandals ratio is comparing than that of Puthalapattu mandal.

Table 2.17 : Education Levels of the beneficiaries of FFWP

Sl.No.	Education	Pakala Mandal	Percent	Puthala-pattu mandal	Percent	Total Member	Per cent
1	10th below	44	88.00	38	76.00	39	39.00
2	Inter	06	12.00	05	10.00	21	21.00
3	Degree above	00	00.00	07	14.00	40	40.00
	Total	50	100.00	50	100.00	100	100.00

Source: Field Survey Data, FFWP.

The Table 2.17 shows that education level of people's participation FFWP. Pakala mandal 10th class below

Table 2.18 : Major occupational Status of the FFWP beneficiaries

Sl.No.	Occupa-tional	Pakala Mandal	Percent	Puthala-pattu mandal	Percent	Total Member	Per cent
1.	Self Employment in Agriculture sector	23	46.00	24	48.00	47	47.00
2.	Self employment in non-agriculture sector	02	04.00	02	04.00	04	04.00
3.	Wage employment in agriculture sector	16	32.00	16	32.00	32	32.00
4.	Wage employment in non-agriculture sector	09	18.00	05	10.00	14	14.00
5.	Student	00	00.00	03	06.00	03	03.00
6.	Other	00	00.00	00	00.00	00	00.00
	Total	**50**	**100.00**	**50**	**100.00**	**50**	**100.00**

Source: Survey Data FFWP.

44 members, 88 per cent, inter 6 members, 12 per cent, Degree nil are working under FFWP. Total of member in the mandal, Village Panchayat 50 people. Puthalapattu mandal below 10th class 38 members, inter 5 members, Degree 7 members are working under FFWP. Total of the people 50 members. Comparing both mandals 10th class inter people participate FFWP, high ratio in Pakala mandal than that of Puthalapattu mandal. Degree qualification people participation FFWP in Puthalapattu mandal is higher than that of Pakala. Both mandals below 10th class 82 members; inter 11 members, Degree 7 total 100 members' participation in FFWP.

Above Table 2.18 shows that people were participating FFWP. According to occupation status mandal wise people belong to Self-employment Agriculture sector Pakala mandals 23 members 46 per cent. Puthalapattu mandal 24 members, 48 per cent. Total persons 47. This sector Puthalapattu is of high ratio. Next self-employment in non-agriculture sector Pakala mandal 2 members, Puthalapattu mandal 2 members, total 4 members both mandal are of equal ratio. Third one wage employment in agriculture sector persons in getting work FFWP in Pakala mandal 16 member, 32 per cent, Pakala mandal 16 members 32 per cent, total of persons both mandals is 32 members. Fourth wage employment in non-agriculture sector people are working under FFWP in Pakala mandal 9 members, 18 per cent, Puthalapattu mandal 5 members, 10 per cent. Total 14

Table 2.19 : Types of works carried out in FFWP

Sl.No.	Type of works	Pakala Mandal	Percent	Puthala-pattu mandal	Percent	Total Member	Per cent
1	Land works	50	100	50	100	100	100
2	Other	00	00	00	0.00	00	00
	Total	**50**	**100**	**50**	**100**	**100**	**100**

Source: Field Survey, Data FFWP.

members both mandals. This sector Pakala mandal is of higher ratio than Puthalapattu mandal.

The above Table 2.19 shows that Pakala and Puthalapattu mandal wise people getting work under FFWP. They are doing only earth works.

Table 2.20 : Particulars of man-days of Employment Generated in FFWP

Sl.No.	Days	Pakala Mandal	Percent	Puthala-pattu mandal	Percent	Total Member	Per cent
1	30 and below	17	34	13	26	30	30.00
2	31-40	05	10	14	28	19	19.00
3	41-50	14	28	08	16	22	22.00
4	51 above	14	28	15	30	29	29.00
	Total	**50**	**100**	**50**	**100**	**100**	**100**

Source: Field Survey, Data FFWP.

The above Table 2.20 shows that people are getting employment days under FFWP. Pakala mandal people getting works below 30 days 17 members, between 31-40 days, 5 members, 10 per cent, between 41-50 days are 14 members 17 per cent, 51 above days 14 members, 17 per cent. Puthalapattu mandal people getting FFWP works below 30 days 13 member between 31-40 days 14 members between 41-50 days 8 members, 16 per cent, 51 days above 15 members 30 per cent. Total people getting work both mandal wise, below 30 days 30 members, between 31-40 19 members, 41-50 days 22 members, 51 above 29 members. Total 100 people.

Table 2.21 : Opinion of the Members about Benefits Received from FFWP

Sl.No.	Benefi-ciaries	Pakala Mandal	Per cent	Puthala-pattu mandal	Percent	Total Member	Per cent
1	Yes	50	00.00	50	100.00	100	100.00
2	No	00	100.00	00	000.00	00	00.00
	Total	**50**	**100.00**	**50**	**100.00**	**100**	**100.00**

Source: Field Survey, Data FFWP.

Above Table 2.21 shows that FFWP programme is useful and their response Yes/No useful to beneficiaries. Pakala mandal 50 members, 100 per cent says very useful about this progrmme. Puthalapattu mandal 50 beneficiaries say useful about FFWF, total both mandal 100 beneficiary say the programme is 100 per cent useful.

Table 2.22 : Other beneficiaries of FFWP

Sl.No.	Beneficiaries	Pakala Mandal	Percent	Puthalapattu mandal	Percent	Total Member	Per cent
1.	Contractors	50	100.00	50	100.00-	100.00	100 .00
2.	Officials	00	000.00	00	000.00-	000-.00	.000-.00
3.	Political	00	000.00	00	000.00-	000-.00	.000-.00
4.	Others	00	-000.00	00	000.00-	000-.00	0.00-.00
	Total	**50**	**100.00**	**50**	**100.00**	**100.00**	**100.00**

Source: Field Survey, Data FFWP.

Above Table 2.22 shows that programme beneficiaries by different categories. Pakala mandal 50 respondents beneficiaries, FFWP beneficiaries by contractors. Puthalapattu mandal 50 members involved by contractors, Both mandals 100 members says the programmes is 100 per cent.

Table 2.23 : Machinery used in FFWP

Sl.No.	Machinery	Pakala Mandal	Percent	Puthalapattu mandal	Percent	Total Member	Per cent
1.	Tractors	50	100.00	50	100.00	100	100
2.	Proclainers	00	000.00	00	000.00	000	00.00
3.	others	00	000.00	00	000.00	000	00.00
	Total	**50**	**100.00**	**50**	**100.00**	**100**	**100.00**

Source: Field Survey, Data FFWP.

The Table 2.23 shows that machinery used at FFWP work site. 50 beneficiaries Pakala mandal villages Panchayat say that tractors and proclainers were not used at work site.

Puthalapattu mandal village panchayat says that, they did not use tractors and proclainers at the work site, both mandals are the same ratio.

Table 2.24 : Type of Wages Received by the Beneficiaries

Sl.No.	Wags	Pakala Mandal	Percent	Puthala-pattu mandal	Percent	Total Member	Per cent
1.	Money	03	06.00	17	34.00	20	20.00
2.	Food grains	47	94.00	33	66.00	80	80.00
3.	None	00	00.00	11	00.00	00	00.00
	Total	**50**	**100.00**	**50**	**100.00**	**100.00**	**100.00**

Source: Field Survey, Data FFWP.

Table 2.24 shows that wages received by beneficiaries under FFWP. Pakala mandal 3 members, 6 per cent, beneficiaries received wages kind in cash, 47 members, 94 per cent, beneficiaries received wages in food grains. Puthalapattu mandal 17, members, 34 per cent, beneficiaries received wages in cash, 33 members, 66 per cent. Beneficiaries received wages in food grains. Both mandal total beneficiaries money received 20 members. Both mandals food grains received total beneficiaries 80 members. Comparing both mandals money received beneficiaries Puthalapattu mandal is higher ratio than Pakala mandal. Food grains received Pakala mandal higher ratio than that of Puthalapattu mandal.

Table 2.25 : Availability of Transport Facility

Sl.No.	Benefi-ciaries	Pakala Mandal	Percent	Puthala-pattu mandal	Percent	Total Member	Per cent
1	Yes	24	48.00	40	80	64	64.00
2	No	26	52.00	10	20	36	36.00
	Total	**50**	**100**	**50**	**100**	**100**	**100**

Source: Field Survey, Data FFWP.

Table 2.25 shows that regarding transport facility in Pakala mandal 24 members, 48 per cent, answered positively,

26 members 52 per cent, answered negatively. Regarding transport facility in Puthalapattu mandal 40 members, 80 per cent, answered positively, 10 members, 20 per cent, answered negatively. Puthalapattu mandal good transport facilities better those at than Pakala mandal. Both mandals regarding transport facilities 64 members answered positively, 36 members answered negatively.

Market Wage Rates for Unskilled Agricultural Labour Compared to the FFWP Wage

FFWP wages Rs. 35 for men, Rs. 30 for women. Real FFWP wages Rs. 55 per day Rs. 120 per guntha (A local measure of volume 12×12×1.6) if we examine the caste profile of FFWP beneficiary, households. It is seen that nearly 44 per cent of the SC household in sample worked in the programme. The ST was 33 per cent for BCs 25 per cent are at wage levels of FFWP.

At the start of the FFWP, there was a directive from the state government that workers should be paid a uniform wage that was the equivalent of 10 kgs of rice at the PDS issue price of 5.65 kgs. This was much higher than the legal minimum wage for unskilled agriculture labour which was set at Rs. 30.36 to in 2000 (Ministry of Labour) the FFWP wage was set at this level in order to provide a decent livable wage. Our assumption is that the main target group of FFWP was unskilled agriculture labourers. Who would have been throughout the work by the long drought condition in the area.

FFWP wages were modified at the village level to a rate that was nearer the market wage rate. In village Panchayat the FFWP wages were modified as the programme progressed to Rs. 120 per guntha, (a local measure of volume –12′×12′ x1′6) dug, even though they worked at different rates in the same village, the scheduled castes were paid 10 kgs of rice per day for works.

Progress Administration of the Food for Work Programme in Chittoor District

Chittoor District is the major recipient of food grains supplied under FFWP in Andhra Pradesh. It is the district generating employment opportunities through this programme in the state. Following tables show the progress achieved in Andhra Pradesh and Chittoor District during the period under study.

Progress Achieved in Andhra Pradesh and Chittoor District through Food For Work Programme in 2000-2001

Food grains in tonnes utilised:	46253.80
No. of works completed:	2206.94
Employment generated mandays:	72,38,587

Source: Data of compiled upto 1-4-2001 and figures referred Zilla Panchayat Dept. Chittoor.

Progress of Food for Work Programme in Chittoor District—2001-2002

Food Grains in tonnes attotted:	173500
Food Grains distributed:	169513
Food Grains utilised:	150.69 per cent
Balance in tonnes:	9641
Proportion of the population below poverty line:	40
Per capita Rice Allocation:	46.4
Mandays (000)'s:	12100
Proposed Mandays:	14583
Total mandays (000)'s:	25.14
Generated man-days:	12051
Prices in 00,000 and quantities in Mts:	12075.64

Source: Data of compilation on 25-8-2005 DRDA office Chittoor District.

Progress of Food For Work Programme in Chittoor District 2002-2003

Allotted Rice:	170097.235
Distributed Rice:	169449.375
Generated employment:	84234
Generated Manday:	227137

Source: Data of compilation on 25-8-2005 DRDA office Chittoor District //www.ap.gov.in//ffw/obst.html.

Progress of Food For Work Programme in Chittoor District 2003-2004

Food grains Distribution (in M'ts):	13140.89
No. Of Works completed:	5485
Cash distributed (in Laksh):	250.323
Expenditure (in Laksh):	1301.594

Source: Data of compilation on 25-8-2005 DRDA office Chittoor District.

Progress of Food Assurance Programme in Chittoor District 2004-2005

Food distributed (in Lakh):	14441.04
Cash distributed (in Lakh):	298.479
No. Of works completed:	7229

Source: Data of compilation 02-4-06 DRDA Office Chittoor.

Progress of National Rural Employment Guarantee Scheme in Chittoor District 2005-2006

Emp. Demanded by households:	2.13252 Lakh
Emp. provided to households:	2.13252 Lakh
Person days [in Lakh]:	
Total:	98.66
SCs:	33.84 [34.3] per cent

STs:	5.6 [5.68] per cent
Women:	54.01 [54.74] per cent
Others:	59.22 [60.02] per cent
Total fund: Rs.	130.01 Crore.
Expenditure:	92.17 Crore.
Total works:	61773
Works completed:	7234
Works in progress:	54539

Source: DRDA Office in Chittoor District.

The expenditure on FFWP in Chittoor District. The co-efficient of average expenditure for the FFWP in Chittoor district. During the year 2001 food grains utilised 46253.80 and number of works completed 2206.94 mandays generated 72,38,587 total funds available in the district 5421.64 cumulative expenditure incurred 2049.98. During the year 2002 total food grains allotted 1,73,500 food grains distributed to workers 1,79,154 rice utilised 1,05.69 total mandays generated 12075.64. During the 2003 according to Data total food grains (Rice) allotted 170097/235, Distribution (Rice) food grains to the workers 169449.375, total completed 5485 cash distributed in lakhs 250.323 cumulative expenditure in lakhs 1301.594. During the 2004 year total food grains distributed in (mt). 14441,04 cash distributed in lakhs 298.479 number of works completed 7229/ during the period FFWP generated employment mandays.

During the year 2005 employment demanded by households 2,13252 lakh, employment provided to household 2.13252 lakh, total 98.66 per cent, scheduled castes 33.84 per cent. Scheduled tribes 5.68 per cent, women 54.74 per cent, others 59.22 per cent, total funds 59.22 per cent, total expenditure 92.92.17 crores, total works 61,773, works completed 7,234, works in progress 54,539.

With these Figures workers engaged on different projects under FFWP employment the heaviest in Andhra Pradesh.

Contrary to the facts programme has been attracting more people from the Chittoor district. It is the affected and drought prone area. Much of the progress of this programme both terms of employment generated and food grains distributed responsibilities of maintaining the distribution channel have been entrusted to one Assistant Block Development officer (ADO) from each Block with following duties:

1. To get delivery of food grains from FCI through main supply Depots (MSD).
2. To arrange transport generally by trucks from MSD to Block storing points (BDP).
3. To contract district and MSD officials for supply release.
4. To maintain monitoring and directing channels.

Other Assistant development officers at each block level have been given the responsibilities of storing at BSP and transporting it to the project sites. Food grains are generally transported to the project sites. A day earlier of distribution as required by the MBO. The local transport between BSP and project sites is arranged by the MBO with the help of Block Development officers. Bullock carts and tractors (if the projects site is more than 15 kms away from BSP are hired to transport the food grains between these two points (once a week fixed days delivery of food grains is given to the MBO from Block storing points MBO with the help of the village secretaries he distributes the food grains weekly to the workers on the basis of quantum of earth work done by them.

Project Proposals and Implementation Machinery

Procedure for getting approval of the project is a simple way in the district estimates and layouts of the projects are prepared and submitted to the Block Development officer by MBO. BDO forwards with his recommendation of SDM who had been given the power of approving by the district magistrate on behalf of the district steering committee.

In early half of the year only ADO's Rural Development and small irrigation, worked out the payment of wages to the workers. Since the measurement of each work and muster rolls were not completed in time due to lack of trained staff, an immediate section was taken up by the state government to give training for maintaining muster rolls, measurement books and taking measurement of earth work and disbursement of food grains to Panchayat Samithis village level workers.

Following Points are Compared with the Work and Duties of MBO

1. There is at once time only one project in a village.
2. Every village has an MBO and he is responsible for the projects running in the village.
3. MBO supervises the Quantity of work done by the workers.
4. MBO Maintains muster rolls measurements books and takes preliminary measurement of the earthwork.
5. MBO has to complete the calculations and disbursement of the food grains.
6. MBO has to arrange that the food grains should reach the village at least before one day of distribution.
7. MBO's are being supervised by different agencies of government department.
8. Files are being maintained for every project at the block Head quarters.

Payment to the Workers

Payment to the village participating to the FFWP is paid weekly in the villages for the projects concerned, wheat and rice introduced the payment, which is made according to minimum wages act which is Rs. 8 kgs plus Rs. 16 per workday. This is rate applicable only to that project. Earth digging work, making culverts, the payment is made in kind and consists of rice 8 kgs per workday. For all other projects where quantum of earth works can be measurement the payment made in kind according to the work done by the workers wages paid before the local market day. The workers are also supposed to do the leveling of earth.

Transportation of Foodgrains

Food grains are being transported from MSD to villages by tractors or lorries. Transport charges depend on the distance. A truck usually carries 100 bags and Tractor 80 bags of one quintal each different rates of transpiration as prescribed in the Chittoor district for FFWP.

Disposal of Empty Gunny Bags

A large stock of empty gunny bags carried from 2000-2001 is lying with the district authorities awaiting disposals. The Block Development officers have been asked not to deal individually, but through tenders at the district head quarters orders have been issued by district authorities to all the Block Development officers to utilise this money earned from the sale of bags in their respective block for making culverts and roads.

Food Grains to be given as a Part of Wages

Distribution of food grains as part wages under the FFWP is based on the principle of protecting the real wages of the workers besides improving the nutritional standards of the families of the rural poor. Food grains should be given as a part of wages under the FFWP to the rural poor at the rate of 5 kgs per manday. More than 5 kgs food grains can be given to the labourers under this programme as an exceptional case subject to minimum of 25 per cent of wages to be paid in cash. The state government will take into account the cost of food grains paid as a part of wages at a uniform BPL rate. The workers will be paid the balance of wages in cash, such that they are assured of the notified minimum wages.

In the event of non-availability of inadequate food grain, wages in kind may be less than 5 kgs of food grains per manday and the remaining portion may be given in cash in the reverse case of availability of cash. The wages in cash may be less than 25 per cent, however, the norms of minimum 5 kgs food grains and minimum wages in cash availability should be maintained as far as possible.

(i) The Ministry of Rural Development will release funds for the food grains directly to the FCI at the BPL rate. The FCI will be required to send bills duly verified by the DP/DRDA to the Ministry of rural development on the basis of statements of quantities of food grains allocated lifted district wise signed jointly by the CEO district panchayat PD/DRDA and district manager FCI.

(ii) No payment will be required to be made to the FCI at the depots by the DRDA authorized agency for lifting the food grains, within the district wise allocation communicated by the ministry of rural development.

Strategy of Implementation

The programme will be implemented two streams: the first stream will be implemented the district and intermediate panchayat levels. 50 per cent of the funds will be earmarked out of the total funds available under the SGRY. The funds distributed between the Zilla Parishad 20 per cent and intermediate level panchayat (and) panchayat smithies 30 per cent. The second stream will be implemented at the village panchayat level 50 per cent of the funds available under the FFWP/SGRY. It will be earmarked for the village panchayat and distributed among the grama panchayat through DRDA/Zilla Parishad (ZP).

Under the programme, the funds and food grains will be allocated to the states, on the basis of proportion of rural population in a state to total rural poor in the country. The government may determine such other criteria as from time to time.

From out of the state allocation, the allocation of funds and food grains to the district is based on the index of backwardness to determined which two indicators would be employed namely the proportion of SC/ST population of the district and the inverse of agriculture production, per agriculture workers equal weightage is accorded to these two indicators.

Ninty per cent of annual budgetary allotment will be distributed among the states as per above principle the ministry would retain 10 per cent of utilization for the areas of acute distress arising out of extra-ordinary seasonal condition. In the event, these funds are not fully utilized the balance will be distributed among the states towards the end of the year keeping in view the requirement of different states.

Distribution of food grains as part of wages under the FFWP is based on the principle of protecting the real wages of the workers, besides improving the nutritional standards of the families of the rural poor. Food grains should be given as a part of wages under FFWP to the rural poor at the rate of 5 kgs per manday. More than 5 kgs food grains can be given to the labourers under this programme in exceptional cases subject to minimum of 25 per cent of wages to be paid in cash. The state governments will take into account the cost of food grains paid as part of wages at a uniform BPL rate. The workers will be paid the balance of wages in cash. Such that they are assured of the notified minimum wages.[1]

In the event of non-availability/inadequate availability of food grains wages in kind be less than 5 kg of food grains per manday and the remaining portion be given in cash. In the case of less availability of cash the wages in cash may be less than 25 per cent and the remaining portion may be given in kind as food grains. However, the norms of minimum 5 kgs of food grains and minimum of 25 per cent wages in cash should be maintained as far as possible, no additional allocation of cash in lieu of food grains will be made by the central government. The central government will provide food grains and cash component to the states in order to generate additional wage employment. There is a balance of food grains from the FFWP the same provided 100 per cent cash requirement is available from such scheme distribution of food grains to the workers under the programme. The state government will either through PDS or by the village panchayat or implementing agency or any other agency appoint it. Distribution of food grains will be made to the workers, most preferably at the work site. In the event of the workers belonging to one habitation and should they choose to receive food grains in this habitation. While the state government would have the option of utilizing the PDS it will have to be ensured that effective safeguards are in place to avoid leakages.[2]

Sanction of Rice

1. The district collector will scrutinize and make available rice as matching share for all the programmes on the basis of indents received from grama panchayat/various department/agencies etc.
2. Preference shall be given for sanction of works where the local bodies are provided immediate relief as per the felt needs of the local people.
3. The highest priority should be accorded for the works being taken up areas where adverse seasonal conditions are most acute.
4. Dovetailing on going works with Sampoorna Grameena Rozgar Yojana (Spl. Component) it is likely that several on going works involving manual labour will be dovetailed with the (Spl. Component) several of these works are currently being undertaken through contacts in such cases the contractor would have engaged labourers on terms mutually agreed.

Therefore, when such works are dovetailed (Sampoorna Grameena Rozgar Yojana) with the consent of the contractor coupons for release of rice will be issued to the labourers basing on number of mandays turned out as on the date in that work. The coupons would be distributed to the labourers directly as per the muster roll maintained by the contractor on weekly basis accordingly to the option exercised by the labourers-cash or kind contribution. The sarpanch shall submit an indent to the collector through MPDO/DPO for allocation of rice. The village secretary under no circumstances will issue the coupons. The coupons shall be handed over to the contractor. The value of rice will be calculated at Rs. 8.00 per kg and the contractor will pay the balance money in cash to the labourers as per his agreement with them. The rice distributed must be deducted from his running bills.

Similarly for other work items involving labour component such as picking surface metal spreading gravel and construction of CD works etc., rice will be issued only on production of muster rolls for actually engaged labourers.

Availability of Rice

The collectors are advised that the present allocation of three lakh tonnes of rice is in the nature of a first installment. There is restriction of the availability of rice each Dept/ Agency/local body can take up works without any limitation on the rice allocation. Further quantity of rice will be allotted to each district/mandal/department basing on the submission of utilization certificate to the extent of 50 per cent of the rice allotted for the works already sanctioned 17.2 per cent. The sarpanch Grama panchayat in addition to the sanctioning powers vested by the panchayat act and rules shall be competent to sanction works proposed to be taken up under the FFWP.

Under FFWP during the year 2001-2002 about 1841 lakh tonnes of food grains have been released to the drought/ food and natural calamity affected states mainly Chhatisgarh, Gujarat, Himachal Pradesh, Maharastra, Orissa, Rajastan, Andhra Pradesh, Karnataka and Kerala. Additional lakh tonnes of food grains are recommended for release to the flood affected state like Bihar. As per the latest report received from the state government/department of food and public distribution against the total food grains of 24.41 lakh tonnes released to the states. So far about 14.49 lakh tonnes including paddy, have been lifted out of which 721 lakh tonnes have been distributed to the states concerned.

Under the programme, the government of India makes appropriate quantity of food grains available to each of the affected states. As an additional and free of cost with a view to enable unable the affected states to provide adequate wage employment opportunities to the needy rural poor. The eligibility criteria for employment has been relaxed as to include both BPL and APL families payment of a wages partly in kind up to 5 kgs of food grains per manday and partly in cash. The state governments are free to calculate the cost of food grains and paddy in wages at BPL, rates or APL rates. Anywhere between two rates the cash component of the wages under the material cost are to be met from the scheme, which the FFWP is implemented the cost of transportation of food grains FCI godowns to the work site PDS and its distribution is the responsibility of the state government.[3]

The allotted food grains to the state under this scheme made after obtaining FFWP district wise proposals or requirement of food grains from the state government concerned, which is forwarded by the Ministry of rural development recommended to the department of food and public distribution for release of food grains district wise. The FCI is to release foodgrains without insisting on payment (from the collector/DRDA) for lifting the required quantity of food grains, within the allotted district wise allocation of the department of food and public distribution. The Ministry of rural development will make payment directly to the FCI, against the lifting of food grains by the states on submission of bills by the FCI to the ministry of duly verified by the collector/relief commissioner of the state government/DRDAs.

The FFWP was started as early as in January 2001, as part of the employment assurance scheme in eight drought affected states. The programme aims at augment food security through wage employment in the drought affected rural areas. As notified by the department of agriculture and corporation, the scheme has since been in operation in the rural areas, which are notified as drought affected the FFWP was later expanded to forms apart of any scheme of the central or state government being implemented for the generation of wage employment in the notified districts. The state during periods of natural calamities such as drought flood, cyclone or earthquake, accordingly revised guidelines were also formulated and circulated to the state governments. The programme was earlier to have ended by 30th June 2001 and has been extended unto 30th September 2001.

Arrangement for Supply and Distribution of Food grains

Food grains for FFWP for the districts are received from Food Corporation of India godowns. Responsibilities of maintaining the distribution channel have been entrusted to one assistant block development officer from each block with following duties:

1. To get delivery of food grains from FCI through main supply Depots (MSD)
2. To arrange transport generally by trucks from MSD to block storing points (BSP)
3. To contact district and MSD official for supply and release and
4. To maintain monitoring and directing channels.

Another assistant development officer at each block level has been entrusted with the responsibilities of receiving the food grains from MSD, storing at BSP and transporting them to the project sites. Food grains are generally transported to the project sites, a day earlier of distribution as required by the MBO. The local transport between project sites is arranged by the MBO with the help of block development officer.

Procedure for Release of Funds and Food grains

The Ministry of Rural Development area to make the allocation of the funds and food grains in the states as per the criterion prescribed and intimate the same annually. Funds and Food grains will be released two installments. The first installment would be released in the beginning of the financial year after the state wise allocation was made, the second one with the central assistance will be released on request from the DRDAs/Zilla panchayat in the prescribed format subject to the condition that 60 per cent of the total available funds/food grains are utilized along with reconciled statement of the quantity of food grains lifted to be signed by the PD DRDA/ ECO, ZP, district manager of FCI. The department of rural development with intimates the quantity of food grains due to the state and union territories to the department with the district wise details. The department of food and public distribution would send appropriate advice to the Food Corporation of India (FCI), under intimation to the union security of the states/union territories for release of food grains from its designated depots under the FFWP.

The Department of rural development will release funds for the food grains directly to the FCI, which will be required to send a claim to the Department of rural development on the basis of statements of quantities of food grains. It allocated was lifted and distributed district-wise and signed jointly by the Senior Regional Manager of the FCI and the secretary (RD) of the state/union territories concerned.

At the district level, the Project Director DRDA will coordinate the release and lifting stocks under FFWP. No payment will be required to pay paddy to the FCI at the depots by the DRDA or authorized agency, for lifting the food grains authority the district-wise allocation communicated by the department of food and public distribution.

Procedure for Allocation of Foodgrains and its Issue by the FCI

The state governments should plan for their requirements for a full year on a realistic basis and indicate the quantity.

They would need during the year. Simultaneously, they should intimate their requirements for each month or quarter in advance and give all the necessary details on a proforma there attached. The union department of rural development would consider all such requests for allocation and release of the food grains to each state and sanction order will be issued and copies endorsed simultaneously to the state government/ union territories concerned. The food department and the FCI, instructions regarding release of food grains will be sent by telex or telegram wherever necessary. The department of food, government of Indian will issue release instruction to FCI with a copy to state government concerned by telex immediately on receipt of the sanction order from department of rural development in case of urgency. The regional manager FCI will also intimate by telegram to their district manager concerned to release the food grains without waiting for the formal receipts of the copy of the sanction order and the institutions from the head office within the allocation made to state/government/union territories under the scheme. The stocks of food grains will be released to them according to their indents from the nearest godowns of the FCI. It shall be the responsibility of the state government officers concerned to see the food grains conform to the standard prescribed for the public distribution system and that only FAQ (fair average quality) wheat is accepted by them. Instructions have been issued by the Union food department to the FCI in this regard not to issue sub-standard quality of grains under any circumstances.[5]

Procedure for Lifting of Food gains from FCI Depots

The DP/DRDA will identify the nearest depot of the FCI from which they are proposing to lift the food grains. So that, there is economy in the transportation charges for lifting of food grains. The district office of the FCI will issue release authorization against the district allocation of the FFWP. It will be desirable if the DP/DRDA informs the FCI, district office concerned about the quantities of food grains likely to be lifted by them on a monthly or quarterly basis. The FCI is obliged to issue food grains against the release even without such intimation if stocks of food grains are available with them however, advance intimation is likely to help in ensuring adequate stocks in the depots concerned at the time need stock once issued will not be taken back by the FCI. It would, be the responsibility of the DPs/DRDAs to ensure that the quality of wheat/rice supplied to them conforms to fair average quality (FAQ). The officers concerned of the DP's/ DRDA should conduct inspection of the stocks before taking delivery of the same to ensure that food grains below FAQ are not accepted. The normal procedure by way of joint sampling as is done for PDS will operate in case of any complaint, the sample from the field will be compared with the sample packet retained at the FCI depot and action will be initiated against all responsible in this behalf, if any discrepancy is established.

Procedures for Disbursement and Distribution of Food Grains under Food for Work Programme

According to the guidelines for FFWP the government of India should make available appropriate quantities of food grains to each affected states. As an additionally and free of cost with a view to enable them to provide adequate wage employment opportunities to the needy rural poor. The eligible criteria for employment were relaxed to include both below poverty line and APL families. Payment of wages was to be partly in kind (up to 5 kgs of food grains per manday) and partly in cash. The state government was given the freedom to calculate the cost of food grains paid wages at either BPL rates or APL rates or any where between these two rates. The cash component of the wages and the material cost were to be met from the scheme under which the FFWP was implemented. The cost of transportation of food grains from FCI godowns to the worksite/PDS outlet and its distribution was the responsibility of the state government.

The allotment of food grains to the states under the FFWP was to be made after obtaining district wise proposals of requirement of food grains from the state government, which the Ministry of rural development would forward. The MRD would make district wise recommendations to the department of food and public distribution for release of food grains. The FCI would then release food grains, without insisting on payment (from the collector /DRDA's) for lifting the required quantity of food grains within the allotted district wise allocation of the department of food and public distribution. The Ministry of rural development would make payment directly to the FCI against the lifting of food grains by the states, on submission of bills by the FCI to the MRD duly verified by the collector/relief commissioner of the state government/DRDA.[6]

— Food grains under the scheme are provided by the development commissioner who also makes payment to the Food Corporation of India.

— Allotment for the district is made keeping in view the sanction/probable plan of works in the district.

— It is the responsibility of the collector who ensures that the food grains as required under the programme have been made available and the FCI possesses the stock according to the estimated demand prior to its requirement. The fair price shops which are allotted this quota for distribution lift and the food grains as needed and maintain its stock so that the distribution arrangement function well.

— If there are no fair price shops conveniently available in the area where the food grains have to be distributed, village panchayats can be declared as fair price shop by the collector in its area for the purpose of this scheme in such a case food grains can be obtained for distribution from the base depot of the FCI directly or from panchayat samithi and can be distributed to the labourers against coupons.

It is also the responsibility of the collector to allot quata to the fair price shops and other distributing agencies according to the requirement of food grains in their areas. The collector will also arrange for payment to this organization for the expenses incurred by them in distribution and their commission at a rate per quintal is decided in consultation with development commissioner. The cost of additional quantity of rice had been entirely borne by the centre and the payment for this was made by the Department of rural development directly to the FCI. No money has been deposited by the DRDA local food corporation office for lifting the rice from their godowns in districts. Where as previously DRDA used to deposit certain amount in food corporation office for getting the food grains on the basis of allotment released, the DRDA allocate food grains to the executive agencies the work of lifting and transporting the food grains to the panchayat samithi or panchayat ghars of the concerned are done through the medium of local FCI depots.

The district collectors would issue rice coupons to the implementing agencies depending upon the works sanctioned under the programme. The implementing agencies would, in turn, issue the coupons to the labourers. The rice should be delivered to the labour on production of coupons only either through FP shops or at work place. Agency from the nearest fair price shop for the purpose as soon as any work is proposed to be taken up under the FFWP. The likely requirement for food gains for wage payment should be calculated and informed and enforced to the civil supplies/ district collectors by the implementing agency along with the location of the most convenient fair price shops/stocking point. The collector in turn will ensure that this volume of rice is placed at the particular fair price shops/stock point to the coupon holders shall collect their entitled rice from such points on production of the coupons.

After delivery of the rice to the labourers the coupons will be cancelled and should be surrendered with due account to the civil supplies corporation or to the person authorized by the district collector. A commission as decided by the government on every kg of such grain moved lifted from that the Civil Supplies Corporation will pay shop to the FP shops Dealer. Flexibility given to District Collector.

The content of these comprehensive guidelines is for the effective implementation of FFWP. However if any difficulties arise during the implementation of this programme, the district is accorded flexibility in adjusting these guidelines to the felt needs of the local areas. Such decisions, the district collector would inform the government for ratification.

The collector will redeploy manpower of any department to the needy areas within the district without affection.[7]

Under the programme as part of wages one kg food grains per manday had to be paid to the labourers up to January 1984. The food grains were distributed directly to the executing agencies. Since February 1984, there has been a change in procedure adopted for the distribution of food grains.

Since December 1984, it has been decided to distribute food grains at subsidized rates the cost of wheat has been fixed at Rs.1.50 per kg and that of coarse rice at 1.85 per kgs. In order to ensure that the subsidies in food grains reaches the labourers with effect from 1984. The distribution of food grains organized only through coupons. It is also the responsibility of the collector to make available the coupons for as many kgs, of food grains as are required on the basis of estimated mandays of labour along with the financial allotment. The food grains coupons are issued to the DRDA by the development commissioner the DRDA keeps accounts of food grains lifted, distributed, number of bags, their disposal. The coupons received are sorted out work wise a separate account of each work is kept. The DRDA has also the responsibility to assess the quantity of food grains available with the distribution and their requirements, the food grains coupons have to be accounted for and dealt with in the same manner as the cash. At the time of the payment of wages to the labourers, recovery has to be effected from their wages for the cost of food grains some times.

On the basis of allotment the DRDA allocates food grains to executing agencies. The work of lifting and transporting the food grains to the fair price shops of the concerned area is done through the medium of lead co-operative marketing societies. The permit to lift and transport the food grains with a list of fair price shops and quantity allotted to such shops is given by the executing agencies to the lead societies. The executing agencies put their demand for food grains in the beginning of the financial year. These executive agencies while assessing the requirement of food grains keep in mind the number of works to be executed and also the mandays likely to be generating in the year. The demand of the executing agencies also include the list of fair price shops and the quantity required in each shops in their area along with the monthly requirement the basis of allotment received from the DRDA and the demands from the executing agencies the sub divisional officer (Civil) issue permit to the manager. marketing society to lift and transport the food grains along with list of fair shops and the quantity required in each fair price shop. It is the responsibility of marketing society to look into the quality of the food grains and collect a sealed sample of the same from the FCI it is the duty of the sub-divisional officer to ensure that the food grains are transported within a week from the date of issue of permit.

Some laboures either received cash or food grains or both only, but in majority of the cases the labourers received only cash component. As such one of the important requirements of FFWP distribution of food grains each manday was not fulfilled. Regarding the payment of wages, 200 labourers were involved in the panchayat, social forestry and PWD sectors. According to survey out of 200 labourers were of the sample only 42.5 per cent received their wages fully in cash. 25 per cent received part payment in cash and were assured of food grains but these labourers were promised to be paid in food grains later on. While in the case of some blocks only cash component was paid to the labourers and they were assured of the food grains component in due course of time. Distribution of food grains is an important to mention that all the labourers of the sample were keen to favour a part of wages paid in kind. The reason being that food grains are given on subsidized rates.[8]

Distribution and Release of Food Grains

(i) The Ministry of rural development (MoRD) will release food grains in two installments to the district panchayat (DP/DRDA under intimation to Food Corporation of India (FCI) and the department of food and public distribution. Government of India the FCI will send an appropriate advice to the regional and designated depots of FCI for further release of food grains to the district panchayat/DRDA or to the authorized agencies of the state government under intimation to the Ministry of rural development and the secretary (RD) of the state government.

(ii) The Ministry rural development (MRD) will release funds for the food grains directly to the FCI at the BPL rate. The FCI will be required to send bills duly verified by the DP/DRDA. The Ministry of rural development on the basis of statements for quantities of food grains allocated lifted district wise signed jointly by the CEO district panchayat/PD (DRDA) and District manager FCI.

(iii) No payment will be required to be made to the FCI at the depots by the DRDA or authorized agency for lifting the food grains with in the district wise allocation communicated by the Ministry of rural development.

Distribution of Food Grains

The national objective of growth with social justice and progressive improvements in the living standards of the population make it imperative to ensure that food grains is made available at reasonable prices.

(1) Public distribution of food grains has always been an integral part of India overall food policy it has been evolved to reach the urban as well as the rural population in order to protect the consumers from fluctuating and escalating price syndrome.

(2) Continuous availability of food grains is ensured throughout shows 4.5 lakhs fair price shops spread throughout the economy.

(3) A steady availability of food grains at fixed prices is assured which is lower than actual cost due to government policy of providing subsidy that absorbs a part of the economic cost about 45 per cent.

(4) The government of India introduced a scheme called targeted public distribution systems effective from June 1997 the stocks are issued under this scheme in the following two categories:

Below poverty line (BPL) determination of the families under this category in various states is based on the recommendation of the Planning Commission. A fixed quantity of 35 kg food grains per family per month is issued under this category the stocks are issued at highly subsidized prices of Rs. 4.15 per of once Antyodaya Anna Yojana-during the year 2000-2001. Government of India decided to release food grains under Antyodaya Anna Yojana under this scheme the poorest strata of population is covered. Food grains are being provided to 1.5 crores poorest of the poor families out of the BPL families at highly subsidized rates of Rs. 2 per kg of wheat and Rs. 3 kg of rice FCI is the biggest food security scheme in the world.

Above poverty line (APL) Families, which are not covered under BPL, are placed under this category. The stocks are issued at central issue price of rice Rs. 6.10 kg of wheat and Rs. 8.30 per kg of rice there are number of other welfare schemes of the government of India.

(1) Mid-day-Meal-Scheme: The government of India launched MDM scheme – national programme of nutrition support to primary education schools 15-08-1995 under the scheme every child is entitled for 3 kg of wheat/rice per month. FCI is supplying food grains free of cost to the state/union territories this scheme is partly financed by Ministry of HRD.

(2) Wheat based nutrition programme a scheme run by department of women and child development Ministry of HRD for providing nutrition food to children below six years of age and expectant lactating women food grains supplied FCI and BPL rates.

(3) SC/ST/ OBC: Hostels welfare institutions and hostels. The Ministry of CAF and PD and the Ministry of social justice and empowerment coordinate monitor of the scheme for providing food grains to SC/ST/ OBC hostels. Hostels having students belonging to SC/ST/OBC categories are eligible to 15 kg food grains per resident per month.

The government of India decided that with effect from 2-11-2000 food grains (Wheat/rice) would also be allotted to the state government at the rate of 5 kgs per head per month or indigent people living in welfare institutions. Beggar home for non-Niketan extra sponsored by the state government and the concerned administration food grains are supplied by FCI at BPL rates. It may be clarified that from the year 2002-2003 the MoCAF and PD has been making the requirement of the state/UT under the head welfare institutions hostels to meet the requirement of the state providing food grains different type of welfare institutions. Since April 2005 the ministry of state and PD has enhanced PD quota of allotment under this scheme to 5 of the monthly allotment this made BPL and AAY.

Emergency Feeding Programme

Under the programme ministry of CAF and PD release allocation of rice at BPL rates districts (Bolangir, Kalahandi Koraput, Malakangiri, Nabarangapur, Rayagad, Sonepur) of Orissa state on monthly basis under this scheme and 6 kg beneficiary/month is used for 2 lakh beneficiaries this programme is mentioned by Ministry of social justice and empowerment of central level.

Grain Bank

This scheme provides grants for establishment of village grain bank to prevent starvation deaths of scheduled tribes. Special children in remote and backward village facing likely starvation out to improve nutritional standards the scheme provides funds for building storage facility procurement of wheat and measures and for the purchased of food grains of local variety for each family. The allocation of food grains was made by the GoI Ministry of Tribal Affairs during the year 2002-2003 under this scheme food grains are allotted to states at BPL rate.

(1) Annapurna Scheme: Indigent senior citizens of 65 years of age or above eligible from National old age pension under NOAPs but not getting pension can get 10 kgs of food grains per month are supplied FCI at BPL rates. Under this scheme Ministry of social justice indigent people living in welfare institutions like beggar homes, orphanages, given 15 kgs food grains.

(2) Sampoorna Grameena Rozgar Yojana: A scheme financially supported by Ministry of rural development in which food grain is supplied to the states/ UTs by FCI free of cost.

(3) Special component of Sampoorna Grameena Rozgar Yojana: Under the special component of the SGRY financed by Ministry of rural development for augmenting food security through additional wages employment during natural calamity. FCI releases food grains free of cost to the states.

(4) Food grains to Adolescent Girls: Pregnant and lactating mothers (AGPLM) GoI introduced this scheme with effect from January 2003. Under this scheme 6-kg food grains per month being supplied by FCI at BPL to the state government for identified under nourished. The scheme is partly supported by Planning Commission.[9]

Rice Distribution under Tender Works

(1) Rice shall be positioned at FP shop or at work place as requested by the implementing agency by the Civil Supplies Corporation. Rice shall be delivered to the labourers on production of coupons.

(2) The collectors advised that the food grains required towards payment of wages should be lifted based upon coupons issued by the concerned executing agency from the nearest fair price shop. For this purpose, as soon as any work is proposed to be taken up under the Food for Work Programme.

(3) Programme, the likely requirement for food grains for wage payment and informed to the civil supplies/ district collectors by the implementing agency along with the location of the most convenient fair price shops/stocking point. The collector, in turn will ensure that this volume of rice is placed at a particular fair price shop/stock point. The coupon holders shall collect their entitled rice from such points on production of coupons.

(4) After delivery of the rice to the labourers the coupons will be cancelled or should be surrendered with the account to the Civil Supplies Corporation or to the person authorized by the District Collector.

(5) A commission decided the Civil Supplies Corporation would pay the government on every kg. of such grain moved/lifted from that shop to the FP shop Dealer.

The normal procedure of joint sampling as is done for the PDS will operate in the case of any complaint the sample from the field will be compared with the sample packet retained at the FCI depot and action initiated against all responsible in this behalf if any discrepancy is established.

The government of India introduced the scheme of minimum assured prices of food grains, which are well before the commencement of the GOP seasons after taking into account the cost of production of inter crop-price parity market prices and other relevant factors.

1. The Food Corporation of India along with other government agencies provides effectively throughout at state, wheat, paddy course grains.
2. FCI and state agencies in consultation with the concerned state Government establish large number of purchase centers through out the state to facilitate purchase of food grains.
3. Centres are selected in such a manner that the farmers are not required to cover more than 10 kms

of brings their produce to the nearest purchase center of major procuring centers.

4. Purchase is organized more than 1000 centers for wheat and 4000 centers for paddy every year in the immediate post-harvest season.
5. Such extensive and effective price support operation has resulted in sustaining the income of farmers over a period and in providing the required impetus for highest investment in agriculture for improved productivity.
6. The name of few states about 41,000 million for paddy and 43,000 millions for wheat Punjab and Rs. 45, 000 millions for levy in Andhra Pradesh is paid to the farmers and millers during wheat/rice procurement seasons.
7. India today produces over 200 million tonnes of food grains as against as a mere 50 million tonnes in 1950.
8. In the last two decades food grains procurement by government agencies had witnessed a quantum group raise from 4 million tonnes to cover 25 million tonnes per annum.
9. Food grains are procured according to the government prescribed quality standards.
10. Each year, the Food Corporation purchases roughly 15-20 per cent of India's wheat production and 12-15 of its rice production.
11. This helps meet the commitment of the public distribution systems and for building pipeline and buffer stock.

Storage Management

Another facet of the corporation manifold activities in the provision of scientific storage for the millions tonnes of food grains procured by it is to provide easy physical access in deficit remote and in accessible areas. The FCI has a network of storage depots strategically located all over India. These depots include soils, godowns and an indigenous developed by FCI called cover and plinth. CAP storage is a team given to storage of food grains in the open with adequate precautions. FCI has 24.33 million tonnes (owned and hired) of storage capacity in over 1451 godowns all over India. In order to reduce storage and transist loses of food grains and to bring additional resources through private sector participation government of India has announced a national policy on handling storage and transportation of food grains in June 2004 for bulk and conventional godowns in the first phase after a series of deliberations. It was approved that total capacity is created at the identified-based depots and field depots through private sector participation and to build own operate basis. RITES were appointed as consultants for the project. A letter of acceptance of proposal of the projects in two circuits has been awarded to M/s Advance Export Ltd., the lowest bidder to complete the project in 3 years from the date of its execution of the service agreement.[10]

(1) The Food Corporation of India has an extensive and scientific stock preservation system. An on-going programme sees that both prophylactic and curative is done timely and adequately grain in storage is continuously scientifically graded fumigated and aerated by qualified trained and experienced personnel.

(2) Food Corporation of India testing laboratories spread across the country for effective monitoring of quality of food grains providing quality assurance as per leading improved satisfaction level in producers farmers and customers (consumers).

(3) The preservation of food grains starts, the minute it arrives in the godwons. The bags are kept on wooden crates/Polly pallets to avoid moisture on contact with the floor, further the bags are dispatched fumigation to prevent infestation of stocks done on an average

every 15 days with minimum and once in three months on traces of infestation curative treatment is done with phosphate.

(4) FCI testing laboratories spread across the country (188) ensure that the stored food grains retain their essential nutritional qualities.

Distribution of Food Grains—Its Impact on the Programme

Each FFWP is to be paid a part of his wages in kind that is, in terms of food grains and cash. It is under the programme, as a part of wages one-kg food grains per manday has to be paid to the labourers. During the year 1980-81 quantity of food grains made available to the states. It was 15.63 tonnes of which 13.34 lakh tonnes were utilized. From 1981-82 onwards, however the availability and utilization of food grains sharply declined. The utilization was 2.33 lakh tonnes in 1981-82, 1.72 tonnes in 1982-83 only 1.47 tonnes in 1983-84 and 1.71 lakh tonnes in 1984-85. Thus during the Sixth Plan period while the total utilization of food grains under the NREP was only 20-57 lakh tonnes as much as 13.34 lakh tonnes (64.85) this quantity were utilized. During the First year of the plan of which the six months were covered under the FFWP the level of employment generation was however maintained. During the plan period even when there was sharp decline in the quantity of food grains district distributed as the quantum of wages paid in cash increased significantly wages under this programme were paid partly in food grains and partly in cash, one kg food grains per head per day was given as part of the wages and the balanced amount is paid in cash. Wages paid in the forms of wheat on all the works, on going or new works that may be started because the addition allocation was available in the form of wheat only.

The executing agencies put their demand for food grains in the beginning of the financial year. The executing agencies while assessing the requirement of food grains keep in mind the number of works to be executed and also the mandays likely to be generated in a year. The demand of the executing agencies also includes the list of local FCI depots and the quantity required in each shops in their area along with the monthly requirement also. On the basis of allotment received from DRDA and the demands of panchayat samithi permit to the manager is issued. FCI or DRDA to lift and transport the food grains along with the list of panchayat samithi and panchayat it is the responsibility of DRDA to check the quality of food grains and collect a sealed sample of the same from the FCI. Moreover, it is also the duty of the collector to ensure that the food grains are transported within a week from the date of issue of permit.

To assess the distribution of food grain component allotted to the works was undertaken. So it is very much clear that there was no match between the release of two necessary components of the scheme food grains and cash only. But in majority of the cases the labourers received food grains component only it is evident from that the release of food grains component was not Commensurate with the requirement. As such the important requirement of this programme distribution of one-kg food grains each manday was not fulfilled this position is more or less the same in all the blocks. Regarding payment of wages 100 labourers were interviewed in panchayat sector. Social forestry, PWD, soils conversation no payment either in cash or in kind was made for duration between three to four weeks.

In case of works done by agencies like PWD, social forestry and soil conservation payment is done by revenue agency in the forms of cash only. Tahsildar and cashier are supposed to make the payment to the workers on the spot after 15 days but it was found that the payment was made for the month. The reasons were not availability of government vehicle to reach the work site and for getting the private vehicle to rent given which is not sufficient amount to hire private vehicle. Moreover, it is not possible to gather all the workers at one place who are near of about two hundred workers working under PWD. Muster rolls are also with the mate so the collective payment was not made and some of the workers remain without payment and wait for the tahsildar's next visit for payment[11].

Limitations on Use of Foodgrains

Food grains allocated shall be utilized for the payment of a part whole of the wages of the labour engaged on the execution of specified works taken up under the scheme. There is no ratio fixed for payment of wages to labour in cash or kind it is left to the discretion of the state/union territory governments to adjust the same keeping in view of the local conditions.

Utilization of Foodgrains

The utilization of food grains was low because of the late starting of the programme as it took quite some time to make necessary arrangements for the planning and implementation of the scheme. As per rice it was 100 per cent in Andhra Pradesh and Madhya Pradesh in two states, where rice was supplied the utilization was 56 per cent and 73 per cent. No rice was utilised in Maharashtra. Wherever there is potentiality of taking up more work priority may be given in allocation of food grains to village Panchayats, over the subject matter departments so that the basic needs of village community are met.

Considerable delay was observed in supply of food grains in a number of villages ranging from 5 days to 200 days efforts should be made to cut down the time-lag at the village levels that there is no delay in taking up the works.

The FFWP started 1977-78 out of the selected states for the Quick evaluation studies. The programme had started only in 6 states—Bihar, Madhya Pradesh, Orissa, Rajasthan, Uttar Pradesh, and West Bengal. During this period the programme taken up next year in the remaining four states. Andhra Pradesh, Gujarat, Maharastra, Karnataka a similar programme already underway under the food grains issued by CARE were being utilised. The utilisation of wheat/rice supplied by the government of India. It was started only from October 1978 the programme was also integrated with Employment Guarantee Programme.

The utilisation food grains was directly linked with the augmentation of financial resources of the state governments. It was expected that the expenditure on the various types of works would be the sum total of the amount budgeted and the value of food grains utilized. In case total expenditure including the value of the food grains was only equal to or less than the financial provisions, the value of food gains released would be recoverable from the respective state governments.

During the evaluation study, data were collected on the quantities of food grains demanded, allocated and utilized by respective state governments.

It was observed that the villages that did not get full quota of food grains as requisitioned showed 100 per cent utilization leading to the conclusion. The demands put forward by such villages were genuine and if given more quantities as requisitioned by them, probably more work could have been turned out in these villages. This leads us to the conclusion that planning in the village level seems to be quite sound for taking up the works according to the needs of the village community. It may be stressed here that, the needs of individual villages require to be invariably met even though we may have to change priorities in the allocation of food grains in favour of village panchayats, as against the subject matter departments who undertake only there on-going programmes without taking into account the felt needs of the village community difficulties faced in the supply of food grains authorities about difficulties experienced by them. In the receipt of Food grains out of the 10 selected states five states namely Andhra Pradesh, Gujarat, Haryana, Maharashtra, and Rajasthan, reported that, there were no difficulties faced in the supply of food grains through the Food Corporation of India. Some difficulties were experienced by the rest of the five states when the programme was in full swing gave a severe set back to the programmes. The same state reported that, the state being prone, floods quick movement could not be possible and the godowns of FCI are few and far between to meet the demand in the flood affected areas. The supplies were also affected due to apathy of the administration and the railways. The FCI could not transport food grains by road, as it is very costly in comparison to transportation by food grains.[12]

Difficulties, Misuse and Malpractices

During the course of the study a number of misuse and malpractices were reported in the utilization of food grains and in the maintenance of muster rolls. Contractors and Fair Price shops adopted not only the misuse malpractice's by government machinery and Panchayat Samthis in varying degrees. It was reported that local bodies like Panchayat which were supposed to serve the needs of poorer sections of the community had also indulged in malpractices in some panchayats in one of the selected districts. The panchayat had resorted to forced contribution for taking up construction activities in the village's inflation musters roles were also from three states. The extra food grains so saved were sold in the open market in one district. It was revealed during the investigation that some workers put in much more hard work than of earth work and as such expected more wages. The state government had also issued instructions that wage should be paid according to work. But it appeared that the agencies in charge of this programme were ignorant about these instructions and as such did not pay more even if some workers had put in extra earth work. In such cases the people incharge of the Programme restored to some manipulation and either put some extra names in the muster roll or increased the number of working days of some workers by strict supervision by the state. Supervisory staff demanded some districts by ways of share at the time of distribution of food grains in one of the districts. Government agencies converted food grains into cash for meeting the cost or material required for leveling and construction of huts. A similar practice was adopted in other district pucca works in the village panchayat this ultimately may result in the reduced employment opportunities.

The contractors are selling part of the food grains in open market in selected states for making extra profits. The cost of the labourers as they did not get their wages in kind at the fair price shops due to delayed supply in one of the selected states. It was reported that contractors sold out food stocks in open market because labourers were not habituated to the consuming of wheat.

Less payment of wages by contractors than provided for in the act was reported from the selected districts and states. When the cases filed in court against the contractors, the labourers refused to give evidence before the court for fear of losing employment as a result the cases could not be proceeded further.

In one of the selected districts the beneficiaries sold out their coupons to the owners of the fair price shops due to delayed supply of food grains.

Malpractice in weighing of food grains by ration shop owners was reported in one of the state on the plea of making food the losses incurred in the process of transportation and storage. They also sold off food grains in open market and supplied only inferior quality. The beneficiaries were perhaps helpless and could not protest against such malpractices because the ration shop owners happened to be the influential persons.

It was surprising to note what food grains which were meant for meeting the needs of the poorer sections in the rural areas were utilized in one of the selected states for purchase of crockery and for utilization in government inspection to slow in the same state, in one district food grains were utilized as well for beautification of the collectorate building in the forms of white washing and painting of building and maintenance of lawn. This seemed to be against the very objective of the FFWP under which food grains were to be utilized in rural areas for the benefit of the rural poor. It would therefore, appear that no consideration had been given in selecting appropriate projects or fixing priorities and the above type of works had been undertaken on an ad-hoc basis only. The government of India should take a serious view of such lapse on the part of the state department concerned.

The supply of food grains short of stocks in FCI godowns when programme was in full swing. The supply was to affect due to the apathy of administration and railways. Another reason is inadequate number of depot run by FCI and slow movement of food grains in flood prone areas. The misuses/ malpractices were adopted not only by contractors and fair price shops but also by government machinery and panchayats samithies in varying degrees in one of the selected districts. The panchayat had resorted to forced contribution for taking up construction activities in the villages inflation of muster rolls was also reported from three states. The extra food grains so saved were sold in the open market.[13]

Supervisory staff in two districts demanded some money by way of share at the time of distribution food grains to the beneficiaries. Government agencies in panchayat other two districts converted food grains into cash for meeting the cost of construction works, such as huts, school buildings, dispensaries and panchayat-ghars and other irregularities.

The Ministry of Rural Reconstruction has evolved a formula for distribution of food grains to various states 50 per cent of food grains to be allotted on the basis of the rural population and 50 per cent of food grains on the basis of last year utilization. During investigation was found out that there was no systematic method of distribution of food grains in various districts and areas in various states. It will, therefore, be desirable to evolve a similar under which the food grains can be distributed to the really needy and backward areas districts and pockets of poverty.

The number of outlets for distribution of food grains should be increased stocks of food grains should be adequate, payment of wages in full be made timely at work sites promptly.

At present several agencies are involved in the distribution of food grains to the workers and there is no uniformity in this system. In some states the distributing agencies are contractors, gang men village panchayat, fair price shops in the interest of uniformity and proper distribution of the food grains and to malpractice. It will be desirable to channelise distribution through the public distribution system in all the states on a uniform basis the modalities of this need to be worked out perhaps it may have to be done departmentally. This will remove the complaints of the malpractices and misuse by contractors and other agencies. There will, however be still need for vigilance fair price shops upon which complaints were received during the evaluation study some of the fair price shops were not supplying good quality food grains as well as there was considerable delay in the distribution. The Food Corporation of India should also be directed for timely supply of food grains. It may also be considered to make the FCI solely responsible as a supply and distributing agency directly up to fair price shops. Timely availability of food grains will remove hardships of the workers as well as minimize misutilisation. Some states also felt serious difficulties in transportation of food grains. Local transportation may be deployed for this purpose. This will create more employment potentioality.[14]

The Major Problem in the Distribution of Foodgrains to the Labourers arises due to the following reasons

1. Firstly at the time of preparation of the annual action plan the mandays calculated against each work are not realistic. As a result, the quota of allotment of food grain made by the office of the development commissioner and by the DRDA is not scientifically determined.
2. Secondly there is no synchronization in the allocation cash and food grains at all the levels state district, block and the work site. For example food grains installment released by the DRDA's. Another important reason for quick completion of earth works is the fact that the BDOs as well as the sarpanches are keen to get such works completed before the onset of monsoon. The fact has also to be seen in conjunction with the discretion that a BDO has for the release installments in a particular work. This problem coupled with the delay of distribution of food grains to the fair price shops, result in either the labourers being given their wages in cash or they are penalized in some cases where the cash allotment has been exhausted.

An important question in the distribution of food grains is the procedure adopted in its lifting subsequent distribution. In this connection told by officials of the DRDA from data of issue of release letter from the development commissioner to the distribution executing agencies by the DRDA take almost three to four weeks. In view of the stock position and in order to avoid excess expenditure in lifting and transportation, it was decided by the chief executive officer DRDA in consultation with FCI to revise centre wise allotment of food grains. This revised allotment was done, but the base center of the FCI conveyed to this lead society that they have not received any communication regarding allotment from the district office of the FCI.

The procedure and processes adopted in the distribution of food grains clearly shows lack of co-ordination, between the DRDA and the FCI and sheer indifference on the part of the FCI. In promptly issuing orders shows as well that it has almost taken seven weeks of time from the date of issue of letter from the office of the development commissioner and yet the food grains were not transported to the fair price shops.

The other processes which are required in the distribution of food grains relate to the issue of coupons to the executing agencies and collection of food grains by the labourers from the fair price shops. It was told by the BDO's that some times the coupons were not available in the DRDA. Besides the BDO's and labourers complained that the fair price shops are at distance of two to five kilometers and these shops open for rate two or three days in a week due to the under staff.

The other related questions concerning the problem faced by the fair price shops in keeping the stocks of food grains for long time, most of the earth works were completed and consequently there was no demand for food grains as the labourers were fully paid their wages in cash. It has also to be mentioned that most of the works undertaken during the first quarter of the financial year were earth work and comparatively demand for the food grains was also very high during this period. Later on, the works undertaken are building work, and their completion takes comparatively longer time varying between three months to one year. The material component is high leading to the situation where the food grains demand is not only less but also demand on the promptness in the release of cash component as a consequence of demand for food grains, fair price shops have to keep the stock of allotment separately as well as blocking their godowns for a longer duration. This in turn upset their other activities like storage of fertilizer seeds etc. Another related question is the state government policy of doing away with the technical section since only administrative sanction is required for the works. As a result of this, there is a great need to change existing system of food grains as there is no inter relationship between the release of cash and food grains installments, type of work undertaken release of installment to individual works, number of labourers employed at work sites. In order to ensure the distribution of food grains to labourers there is felt need to take certain steps both at the state and district levels.

1. The state government should ensure that the cash and food grains components are released promptly.
2. At the DRDA level it should be ensured that the food grains component is lifted and transported to the fair price shops before the release of cash component.

For realistic assessment of the requirement of the food grains both in the new and incomplete works, it is essential for the DRDA to know from the executing agencies regarding the type of works number of workers to be engaged daily mandays likely to be generated etc.[15]

Transport Management

Ensuring accessibility to food in a country of India's size is a Herculean task. The food grains are transported from the surplus states to the deficit ones. The food grain surplus is mainly confined to the northern states; transportation involve long distance throughout the country stock procured in the markets and purchase centers is first collected in the nearest depot and from there dispatched to the recipient states within a limited time. FCI moves about 270 lakh tonnes of food grains over an average distance of 1500 km. Regularly rice and wheat procured in the northern states is moved to far-flung corner like Manipal, Manipur, Kanyakumari, Tamil Nadu, and to the further reaches of the Himalayas in the worth. An average of 1,20,000 bags (50 kg) of food grains was transported every day from the produce states to the consuming areas by rail and road. The Kashmir valley,

Himachal Pradesh, Sikkim, A & N Islands, Lakshdweep etc., which do not have direct link by road.

Thus, by effective planning and management of the transport system FCI regularly moves food grains and sugar from the procuring region to the place of consuming

Provision to Transportation Cost/Handling Charges

The state government will bear the transport cost and other handling charges from their own resources. Any tax charges like sales tax will be borne by the state concerned cash component cannot be used for transportation and payment of local taxes.[16]

Disposal of Empty Gunny Bags

The empty gunny bags of the food grains after distribution of the grain will be disposed of in accordance with the prescribed procedure in the state and the sale proceeds of the same can be used for making payment towards the transportation cost/handling charges.

Reaching every Village—Apathy Way Programme

Prominent among the relief measures is the FFWP, which has received the tremendous response and appreciation of the people successfully put in to action and gaining fresh impetus from the encouraging resulting FFWP is the ray of hope, relief and successors to the thousands who are presently its grateful beneficiaries.

Remarkable Achievements

All the embodiment of prosperity and plenty making great inroads of the drought hit areas. The programme has emerged as exemplary role model in successfully achieving the following.

An amount of rice 677,68 crores has been dovetailed under the programme 5,36,284 works have been sanctioned under this programme. The required amount of food grain is estimated as 15, 76 lakhs mts. The cumulative expenditure has been Rs. 260.89 crores. The number of works completed is 2,82,713. Food grain utilized has been to the tune of 6.02 lakh mts. 882.77 lakh mandays have been generated so far 3,47,415 works have been grounded.

Endeavoring with untying efforts to provide relief the maximum number of relief measures reaching even the interior areas of the state with the assurance of help and assistant. The government has proved to be steadfast pillar of strength. The authorities concern including the commissioner of relief and the respective district collectors of the affected areas are playing a major role in programme implementation meticulous maintenance of wage records and regular inspection by the vigilant authorities with remedial action were ever necessary enabled the programme to achieve acclaim in every corner of the state [17].

REFERENCES

1. Hand Book of Statistics 2005-06, Chief Planning Officer, Chittoor.
2. State Institute of Rural Development, Kerala.
3. Evaluation of Food For Work Programme, Evaluation Organization of India, New Delhi, March, 1987, pp. 1-30.
4. Anitha Sharma, Rural Employment Programme in India, Printed at Sangetha Printers, Mohit Publications, New Delhi-110002,1994, pp.150-168.
5. Priya Deshingkar, Craig Johnson, State Transfer to The Poor and Back The case of the Food For Work Programme in Andhra Pradesh, Overseas Development London, Development Institute U.K. October, 2002, pp.1-40.
6. India Planning Commission, Evaluation of National Rural Employment Programme, Evaluate Organization Government of India, New Delhi, March, 1987, pp. 43.
7. S.C. Varma, Millions in Poverty Grip India Rural Works Programme, Kunj Publishing House, 16, Panchaseela Enclave Market, New Delhi-110001, pp. 96-120.

8. N.5.
9. http://www.sird.kerala.gov.in/empoyment.htm
10. Evaluation of Food For Work Programme in Andhra Pradesh.
11. R. K. Tiwari Rural Employment Programme in India, The Implementation Process, IIPA Indra Prasta Estate, New Delhi, pp. 20.
12. State Institute of Rural Development Kerala.
13. http://www.sird.kerala.gov.in/empoyment.htm
14. Guidelines, Food For Work Programme, Government of India, Ministry of Agriculture and Irrigation Department of Rural Development, Krishi Bhavan, New Delhi, December 1978, pp. 8-9.
15. Priya Deshingkar @ Craig Johnson, n.5.
16. R.K. Tiwari, n.11.
17. Guidelines, Food For Work Programme, Revenue Department of Andhra Pradesh, Government Memo. No:43851/RIF11/2001-03, Dt; 20-09-20001, p. 8.

Distribution of Food Grains under Food for Work Programme

The wages to be paid under the FFWP both for skilled and unskilled labour shall not be less than the minimum wages fixed by the state government under the relevant stature for agricultural labourers as applicable to the rural area. In case the executing agencies do not pay the wages for a category of employment at the rate notified for the relevant schedule of employment under the relevant status, the district panchayat/intermediate panchayat shall withhold further release of funds to that implementing agency and informs the fact to the authority concerned for suitable action against the erring officials under the relevant status and also informs the central government finds that the above provisions are not being followed. It may withhold further release of resources under the programmes to the district concerned [1].

- Notified minimum wage rates to be paid
- Equal wages to be paid to both men and women workers and
- Payment of wages to be made on fixed date in a week, preferably a day before local market day.

1. The payment of wages shall be made at least once in a fortnight. The district programme coordinator and the state programmed coordinator shall keep a watch on the average wages earned. If necessary, the schedule of rates may be revised to ensure that the wage per day is equal to the minimum wages notified by the government under minimum wages Act 1948. The district-wise average wage earned by the workers shall also be brought into the notice of the state council every year Grama panchayat will be the single window for wage payment irrespective of the executing agency.
2. The field assistant shall measure the work done and record in M. Book and close the muster roll at the end of each work he/she shall read out the workers of the work sheet. The entries in the muster roll are to be attested by three representatives of the workers. The panchayat secretary shall submit and closed muster rolls to the MPDO within 24 hour of closures of the muster rolls the technical assistant shall check measurement book.

The MPDO shall issue the pay order for payment of wages to the workers and send it as the case may be. The MPDO shall issue check supplies of material based on M-Book. Where the payment secretary makes payment to the workers. It shall be ensured that it is done at a public place after reading out the muster roll. It shall be ensured that the member of days of work and payment are entered the households job card and the same shall also be entered the employment register maintained at the grama panchayat level in respect of all villages where there is a branch post office within the village, the worker shall be asked to open an SB account postal so that their wages can be accredited to their accounts once a week.[2]

Wage Rate

The wages paid to famine labour are their principle means for subsistence if at any stage or in any works wage rate is very low contribution of such works is meaningless it must be ascertained why the wage rate is low and correct steps should be taken. Monitoring of wage rate allows the district collector to keep a check on the most common methods of bleeding of resources.

Payment of wages has to be monitored very strictly, it really does make sense to open relief works, and make labour to do work for a month or more payment of wages can be either in cash or in kind or both cash and kind in the form of food grains.

Wages in SGRY/FFWP in terms of both food grains and cash. About 92 per cent of the wage employment beneficiary respondents received prescribed 5 kg of food grains per day. However, some wage employment beneficiary respondent did not receive food grains at all. The proportion wage employment beneficiary respondents receive wages only in cash.

Wage Rates and Wage Incomes

The programmes are to be on par with minimum agricultural wage prescribed in different refines areas in a state.

The wages to be paid for skilled workers will be the minimum wages laid down for that category of work either under the minimum wages Act or prescribed by departments such as PWD irrigation. It was also mentioned that the state government might issue an order on the above basis fixing the rate of wage payable for different categories of work to be undertaken under the FFWP. PWD, irrigation, forest, they used their own wages.

1. An effective employment guarantee can only work when the programme is targeted to the poor. In particular the landless, the nature of the work, and

the fact that part of the payment may be in kind contributes to this. The real wage level also enhances this targeting.

2. Wages should not only lead to real improvement in the income of the participating families, but should also have a stabilizing effect on the agricultural wages in the region.
3. If food grains are to from a part of the wage effectively, they must be readily available in sufficient quantity and without the intervention of middlemen or profiteers, these conditions are not inconsequential in India.

The level of wages to be paid to workers in wage employment programmes is an important issue as it affects (1) the level of employment, (2) levels of living of the workers, (3) productivity of the workers, and (4) the inflationary pressures. Different rates have been suggested by economists on the basis of different considerations, some have recommended as low a wage rate as possible, which can be the agricultural wage rate as in the lean season, so that employment is maximized. Others have suggested that the wage rate should be raised.[3]

The labourers in different states and different districts within a state were paid at varying rates of wages under FFWP, the wage rate varied from Rs. 3.00 labourer per day in Nashik (Maharashtra) to Rs. 7.20 per day in Sonepat (Haryana). The female labourer was paid at a labour-rate less than that of the male labourers under the FFWP. The children were reported to have been employed only in three of the selected districts only. It is interesting to note that the wages paid under the Food For Work Programme were equal to the wages they were already getting under the prevalent market rate.

The beneficiaries reporting the wages paid under the FFWP are prevalent market rate and they were of the opinion that the wages paid under the programme were higher than that of the market rate of the wages. The per cent of selected beneficiaries claiming the wage rate under the programme to higher than the market rate ranged from 22 per cent to 75 per cent.[4]

It may be seen that wages paid under FFWP within the range fixed under the minimum wages Act in districts-wise Medak (Andhra Pradesh) however, wages paid under FFWP were less than the minimum wages, which could be due to the method of conversion of food grains wages into money wages. The rate of food grains as prescribed by the government for compared to the market rates of food grains prevailing at the time the other reason for lesser wages, could be due to lesser out put as compared to the prescribed norms in a particular area. Where wages were paid on price-rate basis. As there is no restriction against paying more wages than prescribed under the Act higher wages were paid as per the demand and supply of labour in the local labour market in some districts.[5]

Rates for Unskilled Labourers to be Followed

1. Unskilled workers: may choose payment per man-day under any of the three options as indicated below:

   Option 1: 5 kg of rice + cash eligible as per SSR rates (Blue coupon holders)

   Option 2: 8 kg of rice = cash eligible SSR rates (Blue coupon holders) and

   Option 3: 10 kg of rice without any cash component (Yellow coupon holders).

The price of rice to be supplied to the labour is decided at Rs. 800 per kg if the labourer choose 10 kg per manday no cash payment would be made to him. This is applicable to all over the state in case labourer goes for other option. The district collectors would have to make available the balance portion of cash component of the wage from the departments, agencies to which that work belongs keeping in view the

SSR rates applicable in irrigation/roads building, P.R Departments whichever is less.

2. Skilled workers shall be paid as per SSR Rates they may be given 10 kg of rice per manday and the balance of wages are paid in the form of cash as per the eligibility and SSR Rates by the department executing the works.

In the view of the revised of instructions of the Govt. of India each worker under this programme can choose payment of wages per manday in any of three options indicated below:

Option 1: 5 kg of rice + Rs. 30 in cash (green coupon holders)

Option 2: 8 kg of rice without any cash component and

Option 3: 10 kg of rice without any cash component.

However, for works being taken up under the clean and green programme only 5 kg rice per manday will be given without any cash component.[6]

For the purpose of adjusting the value of rice issued against the running bills of the works issued rice will cost Rs. 5.65 per kg.

The support for the labour component will be given only from the FFWP, 300 kg of rice per hectare and this support will be given only till the scheme lasts FFWP.

1. For deducting the value of rice, while sanctioning the works the rate of rice should be adopted as Rs. 5.65 per kg by all the executing agencies.
2. While paying the wages in cash the value of rice Rs. 5.65 per kg should be deducted.
3. The district collector may choose one of the options prescribed by the state government with regard to payment of wages to the labourers on terms of rice cash 8 kg rice and cash or 10 kg rice no cash.

This would entail payment of part of the wages in the shape of rice to the labour. Since the rate of rice being charged less than the market rate the dovetailing of the scheme FFWP with the existing on going scheme would result in better remuneration to the labour and therefore should act as an incentive.[7]

Payment to the villagers participating in the FFWP is paid weekly in the villages till the end of 1979. Only wheat was being available but afterwards rice was introduced. The payment is made according to minimum wages Act 1948, which is Rs. 156 for 26 working days i.e., Rs. 10 per workday. This wage rate is applicable only, where earth digging is not included in the work like, cleaning of wells, making culverts etc. The payment is made in kind and cash or 5 kg of wheat/ rice for work. For all other where quantity of earth works can be measured. The payment is also made in kind according to work done by the workers. Thus, under the programme a person (with or without help of family members) is required to dig a cubic foot deep pit (locally called khanti to earn a day payment in kind. Taking into account the hardness of the soil the region required 10x8 feet whole same areas 10x10 feet. Accordingly the workers are also supposed to do the leveling of earth. The standard schedule rates for the current year is to be adopted for working out the detailed estimates for any type of work to be taken up under (FFWP/SGRY) the labour component involve is to be shown separately. The number of mandays in a particular work the total value of labour component and dividing by the daily mazdoor rate in the current schedule of rates concerned department of district.[8]

Food component of wage payment and the cash components of wages were received at the work site. Wages were not paid at the work site. Food grains were received either at the work site or through the public distribution system. Out let in the selected districts distribution was only at the work site. While it was only through PDS, nearly 90 per cent of the wage employment beneficiary respondents received grains.

There were large differences in periodicity of cash payment and distribution of food grains. More than three-fourths of the payment were either weekly or fortnightly more than two-thirds of the cash payments were weekly and distribution of food grains was more or less between weekly and fortnightly payment. More than half of the wage employment beneficiary respondents in the backward districts only which is affected by law and order problem received payment on a monthly basis and four beneficiaries report receiving cash wages after 5-6 months. All respondents reported weekly cash payment, received food grains on a weekly basis. But few-reported fortnight payment of food grains.

Special component and calculation of mandays and the quantity of rice required for a particular work. It has been noted that 48 per cent of the selected beneficiaries received the payment of wages every week, while about 21 per cent each received the payment for work either daily or at the end of fortnight. As 93 per cent of the selected beneficiaries had shown their preference for payment of wages either daily or weekly efforts may be made to see that a uniform pattern of payment of wages is evolved in the labourers are either paid on daily or weekly basis.

Regular payment of wages all the beneficiaries reported that wages were paid in time out of some selected districts. But some places where the wages were not paid in time, the wages paid under FFWP was sufficient to meet their daily requirement. The wages paid under the programme not sufficient to meet their daily requirements.

Contrary to the common understanding of FFWP, the programme involved a significant cash component, which was the responsibility of the state government. Cash is required for purchasing material and in some cases to pay part of the wages. The cash component can be as much as 50 per cent of the total out lay and the assumption at the center was that FFWP would draw down funds from existing scheme such as the employment assurance scheme. Jawahar Grameen Samrudhi Yojana, Janmabhoomi in the case of AP as well as general Funds available with PRIS.

Many states do not have ready cash to reallocate or to contribute the cash resources that are required in several states such as Orissa this meant that even the center was providing free grains, but state government were very slow to lift the grains, since the start of the FFWP in 2001. Lifting progressed very slowly. According to report received from state governments and the department of food and public distribution in September 2001 only 1.4 million tonnes of grain were lifted although the provision had been made 2.4 million tonnes to be released.

But Andhra Pradesh was different. According to statement provided by the CMO in July 2002. 2.6 million tonnes of rice were allocated to which 2.5 million tonnes were lifted. This allocation proceeded seemingly in an arbitrary fashion without bearing any relation to the numbers of the poor people or the need for employment and food. Most of the labourers were paid in cash and so few were employed, so most of the profits from the sale of the rice went to contractors and politicians.[10]

Beneficiaries stated they were paid sufficiently of wages under the FFWP. The beneficiaries in some of the selected districts said more than one sources of income other than the wages received under the programme. It would be clear that the FFWP has saved some of the beneficiaries from the centers of starvation the district wise details of beneficiaries reporting the insufficiency of wages and other sources of income may be.

The FFWP rules allowed payments in a combination of rice and cash and this choice were left to the labourer. But almost every where, wages were paid solely in cash and not rice. The contractor received rice for the works from the MPDO through the civil supplies stock point under the MPDO at the mandal level. This was ostensibly done on the promise that the contractor would issue food coupons that he had been provided by the MPDO to the labourers, but the actual process did not work like this and several contractors were forced to make payments to the labourers in cash because they received rice after four months later after the completion of the work.

Rice could not be requisitioned in advance of the works because the rules are that this must be done only after completion of the work. Most contractors received the rice several weeks after completion of the work but they had to pay labourers immediately. They used this time gap to their own advantage some time delaying payment or replacing it with cash. The poor were deprived in real terms because they would not be able to buy 10 kgs of rice in the open market (at Rs. 9 kg with Rs. 56 which was cash equivalent of the FFWP payment. And as discussed previously the FFWP wage was modified at the local level so that it was often less than prescribed FFWP wage in MD for instance women were paid Rs. 30 a day, whereas men received Rs. 40 and two bottles of toddy.

There was of course the added reason that contractors were interested in selling the rice on the open market so, when the rice was eventually received by the contractor they would sell to rice traders. The most common way in which rice recycling occurred was when contractors collected rice coupon from the MPDO and then took rice from the PDS outlet at the PDS price of Rs. 5.65 kg. He then sold the rice to traders who further sold it to rice miller for around Rs. 7.50 kgs. (He then sold the rice to traders who further sold it to rice millers recycling of rice.

The millers finally sold it to the FCI as part of the paddy procurement quota for Rs. 9.5o kg. It happened at the connivance of the PDS dealer, happened the MPDO, rice millers and panchayat officials and FCI officials but the records maintained by the PDS dealer showed that all labourers had taken rice personally through coupons.

Figures on rice procurement for A.P. during Rabi (winter growing season) 2001-02 supported the allegation that recycling was happening. According to Shivaji a former Rajya Sabha (Upper House of the Parliament) member speaking at a meeting on MSP policy procurement was poorer than average at first, but it picked up rapidly later and went up to 2.8 million tonnes against 1.9 million tonnes than the previous years. This increase accrued at a time when production in Andhra Pradesh fell from 4.2 million tonnes to 3.8 million tonnes. Thereby providing further evidence that recycling of FFWP rice had taken place. After the irregularities found during the initial rounds, the guidelines were changed to include the revenue department and PDS outlets. This was aimed at to put in place some kind of checks and balance in the systems. Under the new regime, the MRO was to issue the release order (issuing rice to the PDS dealers) based on the reports submitted by the MPDO. A route officer was appointed to accompany the rice from the warehouse to the PDS shop concerned to (Prevent diversion) the route officer could be the VDO (village development officer) junior assistant. Revenue Inspector (RI) executive officer, the MPDO would have to issue coupons to the grama panchayat and they would have to pass them to the labourers based in their work. The labourers in turn would collect the rice from the PDS shop. The VAO was supposed to oversee the distribution of rice by the PDS dealer but none of this happened in practice. The route officers did not accompany the stocks and the contractors did not give the coupons to labourers, and neither did the VAO supervise the distribution, because of over-stretched timetable of all of these officials. The VAO of MD complained 'we are supposed to do all the things and the continue they would not complete their office works and which was their priority as they asked' "Complete our routine work, which is priority" [11].

Wage and Non-wage Component in Building Works

The central guidelines in order to maximize employment have provided for maintaining a ratio of 50:50 for wage and non-wage components respectively in a district as a whole. In general, mandays generated in a work are the progressive total of person working on each day from its initiation to completion. The programme prescribed for the formulation of annual action plan mentions as an important variable employment like to be generated in a work. The BDO's preparing while annual action plan divide the wage component by the prevailing minimum wage rate for the calculation of mandays. Such a system is quite understandable and correct in case of earth works as in these works there is no materials component and the entire wages are paid to the unskilled labourers. At present there is no distinction made between the employment generated for unskilled and skilled labourers. According to our estimate the wage ratio of unskilled to skilled labour is to the tune of 48:52 in a building work. As such there is tremendous difference in the actual mandays generated and as estimated in the annual action plan. It also shows potential of employment generation in building work which is extremely limited coupled with the problems as previously mentioned such works are spread over for a longer duration, than a year or even more an average due to the problem of installments which in turn necessitates change in the composition of the labourers.

Payment of Wages under the Food for Work Programme

Under the scheme wages will give to labourers 5 kgs per man-day. The state government and UT administration to calculate the cost of food grains as part of wages at either BPL rates of APL rates or any where between the two rates the workers will be paid the balance of wages in cash. The government of India has released 8.5 lakhs M.T rice.

The total fund available now is Rs. 677.78 crores. The districts of Karim Nagar, Krishna, East Godavari, Khamam, Kurnool, Nalgonda, Ananthpur, Cuddapah, Warangal, Adilabad, Visakhapatnam, Srikakulam, Nijamabad, Guntur, West Godavari, Chittoor and Medak are above the state average in the utilization of the scheme.

The districts of Nellore, Prakasam, Vizanagaram, Ranga Reddy and Mahabub Nagar, are below the state average in scheme utilization, are assured of the notified minimum wages.[12.]

Executive Agency

The Annual action plan will independently be prepared every year at Panchayat Raj institution level. The responsibilities for preparing Annual action plan will be that of the Zilla panchayat while the panchayat samithi will be responsible for preparation and approval of the own plan. In respect of the workers to be taken an up at Samathi level. The grama panchayat is responsible for preparation of the own plans, which are to be approved by the grama sabha. The grama panchayat can take up any work with the approval of the respective grama sabha. No financial limit has been proposed as several states have already delegated powers to the grama panchayat and it would be left to the state government to prescribe the same in the light of the prevailing delegation of powers. The work will have to be approved and incorporated in Annual action plan as approved by the grama sabha.

Allocation of Funds and Food grains under the Second Streams from District to Grama Panchayat

Out of the total of funds earmarked under FFWP the SGRY 50 per cent of the funds thus allotted of the district under the second stream would be released to the grama panchayat directly by the DRDA /Zilla Parishad.

The government and union territory administration is proposed to be treated as base for making allocation for each state /UT each year in the future.

The state and district wise allocation will be made Ministry of rural development at the panchayat level the DRDA/Zilla Parishad will make the allocation each panchayat if there is increase number of panchayat in any given year the share of each panchayat would stand reduced proportionately should there be decrease in the number of panchayat the share of each panchayat would be increased proportionately the detailed guidelines in this behalf would be formulated separately. The grama panchayat will prepare their own annual plan for the approval of the grama sabha 50 per cent of the funds earmarked for the grama panchayat would be kept for taking up of infrastructure development works in SC/ST localities [13].

Implementing Authority

The overall supervision of the programme will rest with the Zilla Parishad, at the samithi level, the grama panchayat, the Zilla Parishad will inter will be responsible for supervision and coordination of works and the forwarding of request reports in the states and UT's to the government of India allocation of funds under the first stream from district to Zilla Parishads and panchayat samithies.

40 per cent of the funds earmarked under the first streams will be reserved at the district level and utilized by the Zilla Parishad in the areas affected by endemic labour exodus and in areas of distress as per Annual action plan approved by the Zilla Parishad in selecting the works to be taken up preference would be attached and susceptible to sustainable migration of labour.

60 per cent of the funds earmarked under the first streams would be allotted to the panchayat samithis (intermediate panchayat) 50 per cent basis of the proportion SC/ST and 50 per cent on the basis of the proportion of rural

poor population in the respective panchayat samithis in the districts the works would be taken, an annual action plan approved by the panchayat samithi with preference being accorded to the areas which are calamity prone, face labour migration. Under the first stream 22.5 per cent of the funds will be earmarked, the beneficiaries scheme for SC/ST for providing economic and social assets and for developmental works on individual lands of BPL/SC/ and ST families.

Rice Allocation to Undeserving Areas

The identification of works and the allocation to rice did not follow any kind of obvious rationale that linked quantities of rice granted with either the number of BPL households or the availability of workforce willing to participate in the programme.

Previously, states that each village should estimate the number of labourers who are willing to take up under FFWP. And estimates of works as well as remittance for rice should be based on this but the demand for rice. Interviews conducted in the villages suggest that at the start of the programme, collectors asked MPDOs how much quantity they would need for each mandal.[14]

Ban on Contractors and Labour Displacing Machines

Using labour displacing machines shall perform no task, funded under the programme. For all works, the rates for labour as prescribed on SGR rates prevailing in the area of execution of work shall be followed. Labourers shall be paid the value of 5 kgs rice of at Rs. 5.65 per kg.

The contractor may be asked to maintain a muster roll work wise labour employed by him. A representative of the executing agency should counter sign the muster roll. Coupons will be issued by an official authorized by the executing of the rice component for the wages on a weekly basis, based on which the labourer can draw the eligible quantity of rice from the fair price shop in case there is no fair price shop in the vicinity of the work site, the collectors should make arrangements for supply of rice at the work spot in the habitation where the workers stay, it is desirable that food grains are not handled by the executing agency.

At the time of payment to the contractor the price of the food grains supplied to the labourers should be deducted from the bill at the rate of Rs. 5.65 per kg.

The agreement cost of the project will not be altered due to the dovetalling of FFWP should be used for similar project under the same scheme following the guidelines fixed for respective scheme again deviating the FFWP as far as possible.

The beneficiary can take rice to the maximum extent of 200 kgs per house. The available rice will be computed at Rs. 5.65 per kg at this rate the total value of supplied to each beneficiary will be of the value of Rs. 1130 only for the 200 kgs of rice supplied to him/her.

While making payment for completion of the house from basement of for the rural permanent houses and the IAY houses to lintal level 100 kgs rice may be issued and while making wage payment for the work from lintal to roof level 100 kgs of rice may be issued.

The housing corporation will deduct Rs 1130, the value of the 200 kgs of rice release to the beneficiary from the cash component released by the AP Housing Corporation.

The cash saved by the housing corporation in each coping village will be consolidated and used as cash component for taking up drainage and road works in housing colonies in the same village for which matching rice component may be availed in such drainage and road works, the daily wage for the unskilled labour may be considered notified by the collectors in the districts on par with other programme out of which 5 kgs of at rice Rs. 5.65 per kg, will be paid in kind and the balance will be paid in cash for each manday.

The collectors are further requested to bring these guidelines to all the implementing agencies at district level including the district manager housing for completion under FFWP and fodder seed would be supplied to the farmers 20 kgs per acre with seeds already procured and made available, 75 per cent subsidy and 25 per cent cost basis depending upon the local situation. The district administration will decide the price at which the fodder will be purchased, which will be partly paid in the shape of the rice being given to the district administration will therefore ensure that, the cost of the fodder procured would be paid both in the form of cash as well as rice wage under FFWP as far as through fair shops. Efforts are also made to organize mobile fair price shops at the centers where the rural works are in progress so that other essential item's of consumption also become available to the needy people at reasonable prices.

Since the programme is basically aimed at providing employment to the rural poor raising their economic opportunities and thereby strengthening the rural infrastructure. It is only appropriate that the local bodies are actively involved in its implementation. It is no doubt necessary to exercise a close and strict supervision and control over the execution of works so that the scope for malpractices is eliminated. The programme is with particular reference to the execution of works, stock position as well as the quality of food grains supplied disbursement of wages to workers maintenance of muster rolls measurement books and records.

The progress reported in the utilization resources allocated for the expenditure on the existing plan and non plan schemes new items of capital works and maintenance of the public works mentioned above has been supplemented to the extent of the amount of additional researcher made available to them in the shape of food grains.

The wages to be paid under the programme on a par with the minimum agricultural wages prescribed in different areas in state. The idea behind this provision is that the agricultural activities should not be made to suffer during the peak agriculture seasons. The conditions of minimum agriculture wages is applicable to unskilled workers would depend on the rates adopted for various categories of jobs by the government departments. The contractors have been totally departed from execution of works under the programme.

There were complaints about leakages of food grains in the past because there was no sufficient vigilance at all levels. The food grain the dimension of the programme having increased considerably. In the context of severe drought situation in the country it is only appropriate that a shelf of project suitable for each micro area, in pockets of acute rural employment is carefully prepared for execution on priority basis of block/district wise in each state.

Several instances have come to the notice of this ministry that the payment of wages to the labourers engaged on works taken up under FFWP are delayed considerably due to non availability of sufficient technical staff to measure there aware. The special FFWP has been launched with a view to providing immediate relief to the drought stricken back of delay. Arrangements may be made to mobilize technical staff qualified in civil work from other departments to do the measurement work so that delays in payment of their wages in food grains are checked to the minimum. Under no circumstances delay in payment beyond on week should be tolerated.[15]

Due to late arrival of food grains at the work site, the implementing to arrangements for made was not for payment out of their own funds. This has resulted in some malpractice's like selling the food grains in the market at higher prices after they were received by the agency for distribution it is therefore necessary that there is timely distribution of wages in the shape of food grains to the labourers instance of lack of timely availability of implements and technical know-how for specific projects have also come to high.

The FFWP depending on the availability of quantity of food grains and the priority shall be given to each item of work. The need for streamlining the monitoring system can also hardly be over emphasized. There have been complaints regarding misutilisation of food grains and malpractices creeping into the execution of the programme.

Since the rural poor mostly employed as various agriculture and non-agricultural operations it is necessary that some provided at an appropriate place in the village where the mothers could keep their children while they are away on their work.

Labour Engaged by Contractors can be Paid their Wages in Kind

In order to ensure that the benefit of the scheme reaches to the individual workers, it is necessary that the agencies are responsible for executions of the works directly reach the food grains to the workers. The food grain made available under the scheme can also be utilized for payment of wages in kind to labour engaged by contractors provided it is ensured the contractors maintain proper accounts and do not misuse or delivery the food grains meant to be distributed to the workers. It is advisable that fair price shops be opened at each worksite and wheat for the workers wages distributed them on the basis of coupons issued by the officer-incharge of the work irrespective of the fact whether the work is being executed by the government agency or a contractor. This practice will obviate the chances of any malpractice in distribution of the food grains to workers as their wages in Uttar Pradesh the forest department has been using plastic tokens for authorizing labourers to receive food grains. In Maharastra coupon systems has been adopted for distribution of food grains under Employment Guarantee Scheme. The government of Gujarat has also formulated a detailed plan for distribution of food grains to the workers engaged on works under FFWP.

Wage Levels and the Exclusion of the very Poor and Lower Castes

At the start of the FFWP, there was directive from the state government that workers should be paid a uniform wage that was the equivalent of 10 kg of rice at the PDS issue price of Rs. 5.65 kg. This was much higher than the legal minimum wage for unskilled agriculture labour which was set at Rs. 3036-50 in 2000 (Ministry of Labour) presumably the FFWP wage was set at this level in order to provide a decent livable wage. Our assumption is that the main target groups of the FFWP were unskilled agriculture labourers whose main tradable asset was labour and who would have been thrown out of work by long drought.

For instance contractors and mandal level officials announced during the FFWP Grama Sabha that: FFWP wages would be 10 kgs for men and 5 kg for women. In MD the definite sarpanch the husband of the elected sarpanch, was the local PDS dealer and he was the main proponent of the informal FFWP wage regime because he would gain from it. Although this met with some oral protest, no one dare to lodge a formal complaint against him for fear of not getting any employment. During the implementation of the programme wages were modified further in several instances, toddy was also given, to labourers as part of the wage because the toddy shops owners were members of the committee too or close to the committee members.

The wage rate was modified as the programme progressed to Rs.120 per guntha a local measure of the value of 12×12×1′6′ dug after complaints from stronger (and politically influential) vaddi labourers that every body was being paid the same men and women (the sick, weak, children) even though they worked at different rates in the small village (VP) the scheduled castes were paid 120 kg of rice per day for FFWP works under the watershed programme involving plantation soil work, canal work and bunds, the average income per head was Rs. 56 day.

A major factor was the contractors who were reluctant to pay workers more than the market rate. But, another reason was that implementing agencies with different payment regions found it difficult to change practices and adopt. The FFWP rate therefore different departments used, different measures for payment e.g. The forest department paid by the volume dug and this translated into amounts that were closer to their standard rates of payment in effect this meant that wages were progressively negotiated to a level that was closer to the market rate through interaction between labourers, contractors and implementing agencies despite, they remained above the market rate in dry areas and below it in more productive areas.

Focus group discussions and interviews conducted in the study villages in the end of the first phase in December 2001, revealed the implication of this for attracting the poor.

In the more diversified and productive villages such as the original FFWP wage of Rs. 56 would have altercated some poor and unskilled workers (particular women) but this was revised to Rs.70 for every 3m dug in order to attract more workers. Despite this few were willing to participate in this programme. However, instead of discontinuing it works and rice continued to be requisitioned and majority of the works were completed with outside labour displacing machinery.

In dry areas the opposite was true the market wage was much lower than both the FFWP and the legal minimum wage, especially for women. This created a condition where FFWP wage work was attractive to the non-poor too. In Medak and Chittoor districts as we see in the following section, migrating labourers put off their departure from the village because they perceived FFWP works as a lucrative option.

If we examine caste profiles of FFWP beneficiary households, it is seen that nearly 44 per cent of the SC house holds in the sample worked on the programme, the corresponding figure for ST was 33 per cent and for BC's 25 per cent this would suggest that the benefits flowered mainly to the poor and the, very poor because SC and ST tend to belong to those categories. However, on examining the number of person days generated by caste, it is seen that by far the largest beneficiaries were the BC's in our sample, the BCs were mainly vaddi and mudiraj both upwardly mobile castes and certainly not among the very poor. They have claimed out of being solely dependent on low paid local labouring through seasonal migration it is known that house holds that migrate seasonally are not the poorest of the poor because they have the necessary where with to do so. In fact the vaddis caste council took a decision that labourers who had migrated out would be recalled for participation in FFWP works because the programme offered guaranteed employment with better returns than local agriculture labour.[16]

Price of Food Grains for Purpose of Calculating Additionally and as Wages for Workers

The value of food grains released to the state government is charged by the FCI at the current issue price of Rs.125 per quintal Rs.130 per quintal with effect from 1-12-78 for wheat allowing a margin for handling and administrative charges etc. Additionally to be shown by the state government union territories was earlier fixed at the rate of Rs. 115 per quintal for the wheat. The state government/union territories have the discretion to fix the national price of wheat and millet to be charged from the labour according to local conditions circumstances but the price should in no case be lower than Rs. 105 per quintal Rs.110 per quintal with effect from 1-12-1978. It has recently been decided that the additional requirement may be calculated at the rate the state and union territory governments. The FCI charges the union department of rural development to value of the food grains supplied to the state government at the current issue price of Rs. 125 per quintal Rs. 130 per quintal of wheat with effective from 1-12-78. The reduced rate of Rs. 105 per quintal for calculating the additionally will be applicable from 1-4-78 Rs. 110 per quintal.

In the case of rice, the price to be paid by the department of rural development will be Rs. 135 for coarse (short bold) variety and Rs. 150 per quintal for medium variety the rate for calculating the additionally will be Rs. 115 per quintal for coarse (short bold) rice and Rs. 134 per quintal for medium long bold rice.

Allocation and Release of Foodgrains

1. The FFWP will be allocation based in terms of cash and food grains. The resource will be providing directly to the selected 150 backward districts. The allocation of resources among the districts will be on the basis of percentage of each district in the total allocation of these districts under SGRY. The resources will be released in two-installment year.
2. Subject to the fulfilment of condition given below the cash and food grains component will be released every year to the district rural development agency (DRDA) and district panchayat as follows and
3. Release of initial installment in of cash component is in subsequent years.

The first year of programme (2004-2005) total allocation for the district under the scheme will be released. The amount so released will include the cost of preparation of the perspective plan. This may be upto 10 lakh per district. The first installment of the next year (2005-2006) shall be released on receipt of the perspective plan and its approval by the ministry of rural development and after utilization of 60 per cent of the available funds. The first installment in the subsequent years (2006-2007) onwards will be released automatically to those district, which were released the second installment in the previous year, shall submit the proposal of the first installment after fulfilling the conditions, which should have been met in the previous year. The district which received second installment in the previous year, conditionally submit these proposals for first installment after fulfilling conditions imposed at the time of the release of second installment in the previous year.[17]

Second Instalment of Cash Component

The second installment of central assistance for the year 2005-2006 and subsequent years will be released on request from the DP/DRDA in the prescribed performed as and on fulfilment of the following conditions.

(*i*) 60 per cent of the total available funds, that is opening balance of the previous year, plus the amount received including the state share, if the sate share has not been released against the first installment, national state share will be taken into account for the purpose of calculation of total availability and other receipts during the year should have been utilized at the time of submitting the proposals for the second installment.

(*ii*) The opinions balance of the district the aggregate balance with the district panchayat/DRDA and all implementing agencies should not exceed 15 per cent of the funds available during the previous year (effective from 2006-2007 onwards) in case, the opening balance exceeds this limit the central shares of the excess will be deducted 100 per cent at the time of release of the second installment.

(*iii*) Submission of audit reports for the FFWP for the last year and submission of action taken report on the comments made in the audit report of the previous year. The audit report should contain a certificate from the chartered accountant that while auditing the district account of the FFWP, he has taken into account the bank reconciliation statement and the accounts of all implementing agencies and that advances have not been treated as expenditure.

(iv) Submission of utilization certificates of cash component and food grains from collector for the previous year should be submitted in the prescribed proforma.

(v) Submission of non diversion and non embezzlement certificate.

(vi) All pending progress/monitoring reports should have been sent.

(vii) Submission of a statement about the number of inspections conducted by officer at block, sub divisional district, divisional and state level.

(viii) Any other condition imposed from time to time will also have to be complied with for the sake of convenience, a checklist for the document to be furnished along with the proposals.

The funds to the implementing agencies will be released immediately on the sanction of the works either in full or in installments as may be decide by the collector. The implementing agencies which fail to render the accounts and utilization certificate for the funds released earlier should not be considered for funds considered for implementation of new works and release of further funds.[18]

Diversion of resources including food grains from one district to another is not permitted.

All districts should utilize the funds made available to them during the year that are made available, if the carryover funds are more than 15 per cent of the funds available during the previous year, central share of the excess will be deducted 100 per cent from third year (2006-2007) onwards.

The FFWP funds shall be kept in a nationalized bank or a post office in an exclusive and separate savings bank account by the district panchayat (DRDAs) and also the implementing agencies.[18]

Utilization of Interest earned on Deposits

The interest amount accrued on the deposits shall be treated as additional resources under the FFWP and should be utilised as per guidelines of the scheme. Drawal of funds by the district panchayat/DRDAs shall be as per existing practice only after the approval of the collector.

Withdrawal of funds for making payment towards the works undertaken by the executing agencies will be through a cheque and as per the departmental manual in the absence of which collector may decide. Drawal of funds for any other purpose shall not be permitted anyone violating it will be liable for appropriate action [19].

Release of Food grains under the FFWP Release of First Installment of Foodgrains

In the first year of the programme (2004-2005) total allocation of food grains for the district under the scheme will be released. The first installment of the next year 2005-2006 shall be released on receipt of the perspective plan, along with its approval by the Ministry of rural development and after utilization of 60 per cent of the available food grains. The first installment in the subsequent years (2006-07) onwards will be released automatically to those districts, which were released the second installment in the previous year without any condition. The districts that could not take the second installment in the previous shall send the proposals of the first installment after fulfilling the conditions, which should have met in previous year. The district, which received second installment in the previous year conditionally their proposals for first installment after fulfilling conditions, imposed at the time of the release of second installment in previous year.

The second installment will be released after 50 per cent of the food grains allocated as first installment has been lifted and 60 per cent of the lifted food grains including has been utilized a reconciled statement of the quantity lifted duly signed by the collector, district/panchayat project director. DRDA and FCI district manager should accompany the proposal of any district which does not become eligible for release of second installment due to non-lifting of food grains for reasons beyond the control of the district panchayat/ DRDA concerned like non-availability of food grains of stocks in FCI etc., a certificate to this effect should be obtained from FCI or the collector of the district or the secretary rural development of the state concerned regarding inadequate availability non-availability of food grains and such districts can be considered for release of second installment of cash and food grains together or separately.

The release of food grains will be valid upto the 30 June of the next financial year and in no case shall its validity be extended with the approval of the Ministry of rural development cases allow them to be released separately. If the utilisation of either of the components is not upto the required level for special reasons beyond control. The first installment of food grain will be equal 75 per cent of the total annual allocation of the districts.

The food grains against a release order will be lifted only after the quantity authorized in the earlier order has been fully lifted. The proposal complete in all respect for release of second installment by DP/DRDA under the signatures of project director DRDA and the collector should be submitted latest by 31st December every year.

To maintain financial discipline a mandatory deduction(s) on account of late submission of proposal by the state government shall be imposed depending upon the date of receipt of complete proposal for release of second installment under FFWP under the system there will be progressive deductions for proposals received in the month of January and February 10 per cent and 20 per cent respectively on the total central allocation (inclusive food grains) for the year incomplete proposals will not be accepted. The date on which last information is received from the district shall be treated as a date of receipt of the proposals.

Notwithstanding the above provision, state should submit the proposals for the second installment before 15th February every year. Acceptance of proposals after 15th February upto 29th leap year will be considered only in exceptional circumstance proposals will not be accepted after February under any circumstances. However, if the proposal received in the month of March is accepted under special circumstances 30 per cent cut in the allocation will be imposed.

The programme will be implemented departmentally only contractors are not permitted to be engaged for execution of any of the works under the programme. No middleman or any other intermediate agency should be employed for executing works under the programme. The full benefit of wages to be paid should reach the workers and the cost of the works should not involve any commission charges payable to such contractors, middlemen, or intermediateries no task funded under the programme shall be performed by using labour displacing machines.

In case it is reported that contractors and labour initiate displacing machines are being engaged the collector shall with hold further release of funds to the executing agencies and initial suitable action against the erring officials for misutilisation of funds.

Muster rolls shall be maintained promptly for every work separately showing the details of wages paid to workers and food grains distributed. The muster rolls for all works should have entries showing the number and details of scheduled castes/scheduled tribe women and others who have been provided employment. Those responsible for the preparation of muster rolls should be responsible for these entries also to prevent non-payment to underpayment of wages or any manipulation muster rolls should be maintained in stitched forms pagenated. Muster rolls shall be made available to public for scrutiny and copy of the same be made available on normal price. For works taken up by the village panchayats copies of muster rolls duly certified by the panchayat sarpanch shall be placed before the grama sabha.

Each district shall maintain complete inventory of the assets created under the programme giving details of the date of the start and the date of the completion of the project cost involved benefits obtained employment generated and other relevant particulars. Signboards should be displayed near the works giving these details photograph record of the work may also be kept of the various stage of implementation before start during implementation and after completion.

Wherever required arrangement for providing facilities like drinking water, rest sheds for the workers and crèches for the children coming with the working mothers should be made available and expenditure involved for providing these facilities should be met out of the non wage component under the programme.

The state secretaries may evolve and publish "Rural standard schedule of rates" to eliminate the role of contractors. The collectors should prepare descriptive pamphlets explaining the provisions in local language easy to be understood.

Once the construction of a community asset is completed it will be handed over to the panchayat concerned for maintenance. The collector will decide the responsibility of maintenance for other assets. The state governments will ensure adequate resources for maintenance of the public assets. It is argued, however, that this conflict between the objective of output and employment maximization with respect to the wage rate can be reconciled if it is understood that labour productivity itself is a function of the wage rate. Both objectives will give a similar result of food grains if given as wages and the wage productivity relationship is incorporated while arriving at the optimum. [20]

REFERENCES

1. Guidelines, Food For Work Programme, www google com, pp. 5-6.
2. Guidelines, Employment Guarantee Scheme Govt. of India, pp.1-25.
3. Guidelines, Evaluation of Food For Work Programme (August-October 1-1979) *Final Report Programme Evaluation Organization,* Government of India, New Delhi-110001, November 1980.
4. Guidelines, Food For Work Programme, Government of India., Ministry of Agriculture and Irrigation, Department of Rural Development Krishi Bhavan, New Delhi, December 1979.
5. www.google.com
6. Guidelines, Food For Work Programme, www.google.com, pp. 5-20.
7. Guidelines, Food for Work Programme, www.google.com. pp. 5-6.
8. Mishra, Sangita Dandekar @ Mallikarjuna, Evaluation of Food For Work Programme, Component Sampoorna Grameena Rozgar Yojana (SGRY), in selected Districts Report submitted to Planning Commission, New Delhi.
9. www.google.com
10. Pr. Deb, Strategies for Rural Development Drought, p. 187.
11. R.D. Sharma, Food For Work Programme, A case study of Banda District. A.G. Economics Research Center University of Delhi, 1980.
12. Guidelines, Government of Andhra Pradesh, Sampoorna Grameena Rozgar Yojana (special component). 27-01-2003. Government Memo, No, 71956/RIF.II/ 2002 dated, pp. 9-10
13. *Ibid.*
14. Planning Commission, Evaluation of Food for Work Programme (August October 1-1979) Final Report, Programme Evaluation Organization, Planning Commission, Government of India, New Delhi-110001 November 1980, pp.10.
15. Priya Deshingkar, Gaigh Johnson, State Transfers to The Poor and Back. The case of the Food for Work Programme in Andhra Pradesh, working paper 222 August 2003, Overseas Development Institute, U.K., pp. 21-24.

16. Guidelines, Food For Work Programme, Government of India. Ministry of Agriculture and Irrigation Department of Rural Development, Krishi Bhavan, New Delhi 331-11, December 1979.

17. www.google.com

18. Guidelines, Food for Work Programme. N.16.

19. Basu k. "Food for Work Programme", *Economic and Political Weekly.* Jan 3, 1981.

20. S.C.Varma, Millions in Poverty Grip, India Rural Works Programme. Kunj Publishing House, 16, Panchaseela. Enclave Market, New Delhi, pp. 87-96

Wages under Food for Work Programme

The purpose of this chapter is to analyze the problem encountered in the implementation of the FFWP. For the purpose two categories of data were collected first category of data to the type of works undertaken at block level. This analysis does not reveal much and for understanding the type of activities undertaken at the block level in terms of member or grama panchayat covered, amount, spent in each grama panchayat type of works undertaken concentration of works and repetition of similar type or works in the same grama panchayat. In a gram panchayat two or more school, buildings were constructed. This leads to gross wastage of resources and neglecting other basic priorities of the gram panchayat the total expenditure has been incurred only in the school, building. The DRDA does not take into account at the time of approval of the annual plan the previous assets created under the programmes in the gram panchayat. In the absence of information regarding the assets geared, the DRDA is not in a position to question the inclusion of such works.

The purpose of these programmes is to undertake such work has reflect the felt needs of the area. As explained earlier through the central guidelines a long a list of works could be taken under the programme the state government instructions to limit these activities on items like tank, road, school, panchayat bhavan, well etc. It is well known fact that in the panchayat institutions the leadership provided by and large, from the elite class as such, a high priority is attached to those works, which the community could share. For example while discussing the problems both with the officials and the non-officials in all the blocks the major need of drinking water in both districts, a low priority was given to this problem, the basic need of the people of the gram panchayat has not been solved. This problem also underscores that despite an elaborate outfit of RES personnel not much forth coming from them in terms of rendering technical advices on such issues.

The FFWP was later, expanded to form a part of any wage employment scheme of the central or state governments being implemented in the notified districts during periods of natural calamities, such as a draught, flood, cyclone or earthquake. Now the programme is in operation in the states of Andhra Pradesh, Bihar, Chhattisgarh, Gujarat Himachal Pradesh, Karnataka, Kerala, Madhya Pradesh, Maharashtra, Orissa and Rajasthan for the states/area, which formally notified as natural calamities, affected areas.[1]

1. The collector will get a perspective plan for 5 years prepared for the district basically based on four activities, namely, water conservation and drought including aforestation, land development, flood control/protection measures (including drainage in waterlogged area) and rural connectivity with fair weather roads engaged for the purpose.
2. For each activity as mentioned above the works suitable and required for the area are to be identified in consultation with the Panchayat Raj institution

concerned and local MP and M.L.As. The works identified may be arranged into shelves of works block-wise-and gram panchayat wise. The shelf of works at the gram panchayat level will follow priority activity-wise as mentioned above and within the activity on the basis of local urgency and technical requirement.

3. For each work basic details including rough cost estimate should be given. Works, which can be taken under any other central (or) state on going schemes like Sampoorna Grameena Rozgar Yojana (SGRY), have to be indicated against the respective works. The remaining works, which can be completed in two years, will be done under the FFWP.
4. Works earmarked for the FFWP in the shelf of works may be taken up under the scheme in the order of priority indicated in the shelf of works depending on the resources availability under the scheme.
5. Every perspective plan will have an introduction of the district highlighting the special features and problems of the district.
6. Resources under the programme cannot be utilized for land acquisition. Land belonging to small and marginal farmers and SC/ST farmers cannot be acquired (or) donated for works under the programme.
7. Land development including plantation (horticulture & forestry) apart from the government land works can be taken up on private land belonging to BPL farmers with priority to SC/ST farmer living below poverty line.
8. Road construction will be allowed only for linking unconnected villages and within the habitation with priority to those villages' habitations, which have SC/ST concentration.

9. The state government will forward the perspective plan to the central government with its recommendation along with an undertaking as to how the assets to be created under the scheme will be maintained.
10. The Ministry of rural development will examine the plan and convey its approval with or without modification.
11. After the perspective plan had been approved the resources will be released based on the annual allocation.
12. The ministry in consultation with the state government may permit necessary amendments in the mode of execution agencies for execution and maintenance keeping in view the specific conditions prevailing in a state or districts provided the amendment is likely to result a substantial improvement of the scheme and achievement of the objectives. [2]

The payment to the selected Agency for perspective plan will be made in suitable installments. The last is being after the approval of the plan by the central government. The payment schedule shall conform to the work schedule and payment shall follow the accomplishment of tasks assigned and makes available the data records and documents there of the perspective plan shall be made available in the farm of hand as well as electronic copies. The amount to be paid shall be decided as per the general guidelines as may be issued by state government (or) central government.

The size of the works undertaken permits employment to a handful of labourers. Coupled with the problems of allotment labourers are employed over a period of one year by earth works; by and large the works are completed in a very short period varying between one week to four weeks at the most. This is possible because of prompt allotment as well as larger numbers of labourers are employed for its completion. In earth works payments are made at piece rate basis. Entire family including children used to be engaged in the some works, in most of the earth works the labourers were engaged in two shifts it is also interesting to note that in most of the places where the work was in progress, the labourers did not allow the out sides work. It also came to our notice to such work the sarpanches by and large employ their own persons. The employment opportunities are very limited and the wages given in the programme are much higher than the prevailing market wage rate.

As and when and where it is required works from the shelf of works of the gram panchayat concerned can be taken up. The works can be got executed from line departments PRIs/reputed NGO's/Self-help-groups/other agencies of central (or) state government as may be decided by the collector. The collector, before entrusting any work to any executing agency shall get an undertaking from the agency concerned to maintain separate account, make available records for audit and inspection cooperate and follow the guidelines of the scheme. The agencies violating the undertaking should not violate the undertaking should not be considered for further releases of funds and the money already advanced shall be recovered if violation of very serious nature like use of labour displacing machines cost escalations beyond specified limits diversion of funds etc. [3]

Wherever watersheds/water user committees are not constituted formally, the works can be executed by the user groups consisting of stakeholder for a given work structure. Necessary sanction may be accorded as per existing of the state government.

Before examining the implementation process in FFWP, it is necessary to describe briefly the administrative set up, so as to get a close look at the agencies executing the programme. Basically the following agencies are involved in the implementation of the programme:

— Department of panchayat and rural development
— Rural engineering services
— Collector district development officer
— District rural development agency and
— Panchayat and institutions.

Strengthening of the Technical and Administrative Setup at the Block Level

Though it is difficult to say as to what should be the optimum size of the technical unit in the block. It may be observed that the present technical set up is inadequate to supervise all the work that is under the programme. It should be strengthened to supervise the on-going works effectively. The engineering cell should be streamlined and oriented to the system of departmental execution of works as against the contract system. In order to facilitate the monitoring and feed back, the administrative set up at the block level has to be strengthened. It is suggested to create a post of progress assistant whose only duty will be to prepare necessary feed back after monitoring the on-going projects particularly relating to FFWP. [4]

Upto one per cent of funds can be used for contingencies and will include monitoring and training reported to the Ministry of rural development at the time of second installment.

Each executing agency shall maintain an employment register. The works being implemented within its jurisdiction under its own component which would contain the details like number of persons employed including the number of SC/ST, gender of the workers and number of man days generated for each work under the FFWP. This information should be based on the muster rolls to be maintained work-wise. This register would be open to the public for scrutiny. Copies of this register shall be made available to public on demand after charging a small fee necessary. The state shall fix the fee. Display board should be put on the work site giving details of the work. Photographs of the works at various stages may be displayed as well.

The collector may compile and consolidate information regarding generating of man days and expenditure of works activity-side at the block and the district level for which it need be, outsourcing of man power may be done by using funds for contingency earmarked under the programme.

District Rural Development Agency

The main functions of the DRDA with record to the FFWP are as follows.

1. Approval of Annual action plan pertaining to blocks and other agencies.
2. Release of grant to blocks/agencies with the approval of the collector, the state government took a decision to disburse through the DRDA's. Now this amount is debited in DRDA (Personal Deposit Account).
3. Distribution of food grains with the FCI on the one hand and leads and link societies on the other.

At the district level the collector is responsible for the implementation of this programme. Collector is the chairman of the DRDA specifically to the FFWP District development officer on behalf of the collector functions for matters connected with the administrative approval and monitoring of the programme, the DDO performs the following functions: [5]

Administrative approval of all the works which are normally sanctioned by the collector requires an examination of the works on behalf of the collector. Review the progress every month in a meeting presided over by the collector and attended by executive engineer (RES) and distribution of food grains to the block and other executive agencies.

The district collectors are requested to take up this programme as mission to provide relief and employment to the people affected by drought. The district collectors should ensure that the departments government corporations/ agencies, local bodies, market committees, habitation committees and NGO's are fully involved in the implementation of the programme. The government has already allocation 3.0 lakh tonnes of rice to the affected districts. The government of India had sanctioned additional quantity of rice. The district collector should accordingly workout action plan for utilizing this quantity of rice under the programme in order to keep the momentum and continuity of the programme to provide relief in the drought affected districts. The works under FFWP are permitted to be taken up in rural areas to all 22 districts.

Collectors obtain guidelines of the districts level committee of political parties. The expanded guidelines should be circulated to all the public representatives in order that they are freely aware of the programme. The collectors shall constitute district level committee of political parties presided over by the local minister as designated in officials committees at mandal level and gram panchayat level would be constituted by collectors for reviewing the relief activities constituted out here under, as a mandal level. Mandal Parishad, ZPTC, member. MRO, MPDO, AEPr, AE, RWS, as members panchayats level gram panchaayat Sarpanch to preside over by a sarpanch MPTC member, VAO, VDO, a few leaders of self-help groups as members.

All the district collectors are requested to convey a review meeting immediately with the district level officers concerned and identify the funds available at the district level for utilizing the food grains available under FFWP. The collectors should also identify all ongoing works of the departments of the forest and irrigation; market; committee ZPP; MPP; village panchayat etc. and see that, they generate extra works with the amounts saved by utilisation of rice on all such ongoing works. The rice allocated to the worker beneficiary is in lieu of cash but not as an additional.

Development works water harvesting digging or desilting of ponds and tanks, manually construction of rural link roads, to upgrade earthen roads as metal roads along with side drainage within the village funds any material component can be sanctioned from any scheme and rice towards wage component can be drawn from FFWP. Increasing the volume of works of all the departments, where labour component involved all works taken up under the FFWP.

Horticulture crops and plantations involving substantial labour component can be taken up. The programme can also be extended to leveling improving of land allotted in the past for house sites, which have so far not been developed strengthen repairs and construction of bridges and feeder channels irrigation cannals to irrigation sources.

In dark grey areas and in stress areas identified by under ground, under development, where recharge the water table is most important, the construction of farm ponds/percolations tanks on private lands can be taken. The works relating to the extension of pipelines and drinking water distribution systems are also eligible for coverage under this programme. Andhra Pradesh rural development houses, under the scheme of rural permanent houses are also eligible to draw up to 200 kgs per house. The department of animal husbandry could dovetail FFWP with the scheme to raise fodder community lands together with a plan and buy back distribution of such fodder. The maintenance of roads being undertaken by the roads and building department could be dovetailed with the FFWP especially in labour intensive works such as clearance of shrubs and maintenance. [6]

At the state level, the department of panchayat and rural development has got overall responsibility in the policy and implementation of this programme. To this end, this department issues from time to time various instructions touches almost all the important aspects of this programme from planning to implementation, finance and monitoring and inter-relationship between the executing agencies.

Panchayat Institutions

Provided for a gram panchayat at the village level, panchayat at the block level and a Zilla panchayat at the district level. This act is a comprehensive document and covers the entire field of local self-government through out the state. The panchayats are empowered to deal with several aspects of civic life of the rural population and in some cases have are required to do such more than the municipal bodies.

Besides Janapada Panchayat is also charged and implementation of development plans charged with specific executive responsibility in fields like primary education, health, sanitation and communication. The gram panchayat at the village level is the basic institution for planning and executing the development programmes.

Machinery for Implementation of the Programme

Steering committee has been set up to implement the programme both at state and district levels. At the state level the chief secretary or development commissioner or any other senior secretary of the state governments heads the committee. Secretaries and heads of departments operating the scheme or having potentialities of participations are represented in the committee. A representative of the department of rural reconstruction government of the senior regional manager of Food Corporation of India is also a member of the state steering committee.

Likewise, at the district level the steering committee headed by the district magistrate is collector. The departmental heads concerned with the works taken up in the district under the programme. The committee also has representatives of Zilla parishad/district panchayat if such as a selected body is functioning in the district.

The main task of the steering committee is to plan to the works that to be taken up under the programme and see that the progress of these works is not allowed to suffer for any reason. The senior regional manager FCI plan supplier in such a manner that there are no bottlenecks anywhere the supply of food grains and works under this programme do not suffer that want of food grains in any case.

India will undertake a structured random check of the assets created under the FFWP. This service known as rural engineering service it was created primarily due to the reason that in executing local development works in rural areas, experience indicated that technical guidance is necessary for the execution and maintenance of such works, normally before the creation of RES a sub-engineer was appointed in every development block but there was no arrangement for inspecting the work of the sub-engineer and to provide him the necessary guidance. The RES was constituted with a view of implementing small scheme in rural areas, with the following objectives:

1. To exercise technical control on all construction work of under the FFWP and other department programmes in the jurisdiction of the panchayats and render technical guidance and advices to the local authorities for planned execution of these works.
2. To execute and finalize construction work of other departments of the state government. The superintending engineer with his auxiliary staff in the office of the development commissioner is available to the village panchayats for construction works at the state level. There is an executive engineer at the divisional level and two assistant engineers at the district level and two sub-engineers. In each development block in order to oversee that the construction works are executed in a well planned way and technical and financial control is duly exercised on these works. The government from time

to time had taken decisions and issued orders as here under.

3. The public works department manual and the central public works account code are applicable to all construction work undertaken by this service so that technical and financial control is maintained and the account is audited by the accounted general. All the executive engineers in this service have been declared drawing and disbursing officers.
4. In order that all-technical and financial and administrative duties that are entrusted to their service are completed during the specified period. Every executive engineer and the assistant engineer have been given technical office staff corresponding with the officers of the other technical departments.
5. In order that the construction works are executed strictly in accordance with relevant specifications. The technical guidebooks published by department of panchayat and rural development have been made applicable to all construction works. [7]
6. All executive engineers have been declared heads of their officers.
7. For close technical control in remote places of rural areas and timely inspection of all construction works, executive engineers have been sanctioned. The service so that they may carry out a detailed inspection of the works.
8. So far as the works within the jurisdiction of panchayat areas are concerned, the procedure is already fixed. According to all construction the block development officer through the grama panchayat executes works of the panchayat. These works are executed through contract and the accounts of these are maintained by the block development officer for which BDO's are fully responsible.

9. But in the case of minor irrigation the RES executes works and construction works of other departments costing to two lakh in rural areas and their maintenance directly. For these works the procedure to be followed is as prescribed by the state government. For corresponding works of other technical department other words all these works shall be executed departmentally or by contract after obtaining administrative approval and technical sanction.

The main purpose was that the construction works of any amount may not only be executed properly, but also are subject to strict technical and financial control. Keeping this in view, the administration structure of this service similar to the obtaining for officers of the divisional, district and other levels under the directorate of panchayat and rural development in other words administratively. The executive engineer, the assistant engineer and the sub- engineers shall work under the Divisional Commissioner, the district collector and the BDO respectively in respect of works of other department they retain their entity like the corresponding officers of other technical department. The executive engineer is responsible for their pay, travel allowances etc and the assistant engineer for the staff under him and the assistant engineer for the staff as well as the sub-engineer. The pay and allowances of the sub-engineers are disbursed through the reported to BDO's. The tour programme of the assistant engineer is approved by the executive engineer.

It is evident from the above the officers of the RES have to shoulder dual responsibility. While in respect of construction works under the jurisdiction of the panchayats, the sub-engineer is responsible to the BDO assistant engineer to the collector on the one hand without prejudice to the local administration primary on the other, the sub-engineer is responsible to the assistant engineer, the assistant engineer to the executive engineer and the executive engineer to the development commissioner. [8]

1. At the village level gram panchayat shall be principal authority for planning implementation of the scheme. The gram panchayat (GP) shall be responsible for identification of the works in the gram panchayat area as per the recommendation of the gram sabha and ward sabhas and for executing supervising such works.
2. The panchayat secretary shall be responsible for receiving applications for registration and issue of job cards. The field assistant to assist the panchayat secretary in maintaining the records and also to assist in technical assistant is being provided at the mandal level.
3. At the mandal level, the mandal Parishad shall be the principal authority for planning and implementation of the programme and assist the gram panchayat and the mandal Parishad in carrying out its functions under the scheme. The MPDO shall be provided with additional support of three technical assistants two from engineering and one from the agriculture department and one accountant and computer assistant to provide technical support to gram panchayat.
4. There shall be a programme officer for each mandal level. The programme officer will be a full time officers he may be taken on deputation. The Programme officer has a critical role in coordinating at the mandal level. He will be responsible for scrutinizing village EGS plan ensuring that they match work with employment demand, that implementing agencies start works on time, that the employment demand is met within time and workers receive their due amoluments. Among his important functions are ensuring the social audit by the gram sabha, disposing complaints and grievances redressed the programme officer will assist the mandal Parishad

in its functions under the scheme the programme officer shall function under the direction, control and superintendence of the district programme coordinator and will also be accountable to the mandal parishad. One accountant cum-computer assistant shall assist the programme officer.

5. The mandal samakya federation of the village organization of the poor will be responsible for the mobilization of the wage seekers through the village organizations and SHG's to assess their rights and entitlements provided under the scheme in addition the mandal samakya may assist the programme. Officer in handling information, education and communication activities relating to the scheme mandal samakya will be facilitated to engage a social organizer to support themes in a carrying out these functions.
6. At the district level, the Zilla Parishad shall be the principal authority for planning and implementation of the scheme. The Zilla Parishad shall approve the district Employment Guarantee Scheme, which includes the consolidated mandal EGS plans its own proposals and project proposals received from other line departments. It shall also review the programme implementation supervise and monitor projects taken up at the district and mandal level in agency areas. The governing body of ITDA shall function along with Zilla Parishad.
7. The district collector shall be the district programme co-ordinator for the implementation of the scheme in the district. There shall be an employment guarantee scheme established in the office of the project director DWMA, chief executive officer, S.P. Project Director, DRDA and Project officer, ITDA (in agency area) as additional district programme co-coordinator the PD DWMMA shall assist the DPC in overall management

of the scheme. The CEOZP shall assist the DPC in implementation of the scheme by the PRIS. The PDDRDA shall assist the DPC in the mobilization of wage seeking families through the self-help group of women and their federations at village, mandal and district level. The Programme officer ITDA shall assist the DPC in the management of the scheme in the agency areas.

8. At the state level, the commissioner, rural development (CRD) shall be the state programme co-coordinator (SPC) he/she shall be assisted by an FFWP unit consisting of a director and a subject specialist and support staff.
9. The commissioner, panchayat Raj shall co-ordinate the implementation of the scheme with the Panchayat Raj institutions (PRI).
10. The chief executive officer, society for elimination of rural poverty (SERP) shall ensure. The involvement of DRDAs in mobilization and capacity building of the wage seeking families through the self-help groups of women and their federations at the village, mandal and district level.
11. The commissioner, tribal welfare shall ensure the involvement of ITDAs in implementation of the scheme in agency areas.
12. The commissioner AMR-Apard shall provide capacity building support to the PRIs and the line departments.
13. The managing director APSC co-operative finance corporation Ltd., shall ensure the involvement of districts SC service co-operative societies in enabling the scheduled castes households to access their rights and entitlements particularly in development of their lands with irrigation facilities.
14. State government shall make rules to carryout the provisions of the act pertaining to state responsibilities

under the Act 32 (1) the state government shall set up the employment guarantee fund provide budget provision for and release the state share, notify rural SSR from time to time, conduct impact assessment and evaluation studies. The state government shall set up Andhra Pradesh State Employment Guarantee Council (APSEGC) under section 12(1) of the act. The APSEGS shall be the advisory body for the purpose of the AP rural employment programmes it shall have chief minister as chairman rural development minister as vice-chairman principal secretary (rural development) as member convenor, with 15 non-officials and 8 officials as members.

15. Non-Government Organization shall be involved as partners in community mobilization, capacity, social audit and monitoring of processes relating to right and entitlement of the works.[9]

Social Audit and Vigilance at Grassroots Level

For every work sanctioned under this scheme there will be a monitoring committee of the villages of the area to monitor the progress and quality.

— Every such committee shall have 5 to 9 members from the social workers, retired civil defense or private sector officials, other retired employees like teachers, well educated persons, an SC, ST and women representatives.

— The monitoring committee will be constituted in the meeting of local beneficiaries convened by the local member of gram panchayat.

— The work cannot be started without constitution of monitoring committee.

— Monitoring committee would be appraised by the implementing agency about the estimate time frame and quality parameters of the works.

The final report of the committee would be attached along with the completion of certificate.

The awareness of FFWP wide publicity through audio, Video, Kalajatha press and wall writing is taken up in the selected districts.

A family card has been issued to the identified labourer in the each habitation for maintaining the records regarding supply of rice, cash and number of workdays.

Operationalisation Problems

It is true that the programme is both an instrument of capital formulation and building infrastructure. But the limitation is that the programme is dependent on surplus food stock that in turn is totally dependent on the several of monsoon drought affected areas. The government, to be precise, has declared the whole state as drought affected area, if we review the food production in India; the results are not highly encouraging. India today faces grave and gram situation in population per year itself requires additional one million tonnes of food grains. Thus, divergent trends between increasing population and more or less stagnant agricultural productions quite clear, slowly and gradually with the passage of time.[10]

Problems Faced by Implementers

Some of the problems faced by implementers, specially at the district and taluka levels, are as follows: (1) shortage of staff, (2) problems of coordination, (3) problems pertaining to the 60:40 labour material ratio, (4) timely supplies of food grains, (5) non-availability of enough workers and their irregular supply, and interference of non-officials. The first problem has already been examined. The second problem of coordination originates from a number of factors.

(1) ATDO is not on a higher scale than deputy is engineer is and DRDA director is not superior to an executive engineer in the bureaucratic hierarchy. The

horizontal and vertical linkages, therefore, clash and this does not allow the DRDA director to coordinate the implementation work. A strong taluka panchayat president or an active involvement of the DRDA may be able to help DRDA director does not have enough control over the functioning of panchayat officers. As the later belongs to the panchayat hierarchy, while the former does not interference of non-officials also created problems are neither the TDO nor the DRDA director is in a position to assert himself. When it comes to dealing with non-officials (4) poor co-ordination is also due to the poor planning component of the NREP/FFWP. Lack of systematic planning leaves wide scope for adhocism and manipulation, which are likely to be misused. Though there is no easy solution to the above problem we feel that the strengthening of planning for the FFWP/NREP is likely to be of help substantially as it will leave lesser scope for manipulation.

As regards the third problem pertaining to the 60:40 labour material ration (50: 50) it was observed that on the hand some implementers found it difficult to spend the material component while on the other hand, other implementers used various ways to reduce the material component of FFWP/DRDA works in the former case the result was non-durable assets, while in the latter case some times unfair practices were observed. The district frequently faced the problems of non-durable assets.

It was frequently complained that FFWP works were not taken up in some areas because workers were not available and even they were available their supply was not regular. Interestingly such complaints came from FFWP/DRDA a number of migrant workers works on NREP works our study showed that there are several reasons for this: firstly the administering does not spend much time and energy on the extension work of the FFWP second, no estimates are made regarding the exact nature of unemployment and, consequently, planners do not know about the workers are available and their performances while planning for FFWP. Thirdly workers are not assured of continuous employment, as it is not planned in such a way. Lastly the non-officials are relatively better off more enlightened and they attract a number of FFWP workers as well as migrant workers to their areas.

The non-availability of workers especially in the tribal and backward areas and which desperately need infrastructure facilities appears to be due to the lack of efforts and systematic planning.

Another problem faced by the implementations of food grains. This seemed to be a problem of coordination. The district level committee for the FFWP, also the deputy engineer as its members should have been able to arrange for timely and easy availability of supplies. But this did not seem to be happening very often-labourers had to travel up to the MRO office to get coupons and or food grains they again go back for grinding the grains and in the process remain away from work for a day or two the quality of food grains in all the four places where we received complaints and observed the food grains was of very poor quality. Although the responsibility for the poor quality would be rested with the FCI the DRDA office. The panchayat president returned such bad quality food grain and procured reasonably good quality grains.

In short, the problems faced by implementers are important in the sense that, if they are not solved, they are likely to have an adverse impact in rural areas. However except for the shortage of staff all other major problems can be solved to a great extent by systematic planning and by improving coordination between the civil supply department and the rural panchayat administration.

Problems in Implementation

Chief Minister set out the following major issues, which have come to his notice from time to time.

1. Food grains were not available in time a part from the difficulty in overall availability of food grains many fair price shop dealers were not interested in lifting, as the margin commission was not attractive. There was certain inaccessible area where transport of the food grains costs heavy let alone unforeseen risks.
2. Funds are given for specific items for creating of durable assets persons can be given the work under the programme, but a large number of women and children go to the work spots.
3. A proper assessment of the work is yet to be made. There is no doubt some difficulties because the work out numbers village level functionaries.
4. Through overall availability of funds has been ensured the state level funds do not reach in time. As a consequence of the uncertainty of flow of funds, the works were not showing uniform progress all through the year.
5. It is extremely necessary that proper preparations are made from now onwards for meeting the situation which will emerge in the months of April and May. These were always difficult months and in past there many were cases of starvation deaths at too during the lean season, in some scarcity pockets. The pockets should be identified so that food for works may be taken up early. Fortunately owing to a large number of works taken up there were not reports of starvation deaths.
6. Problems arose due to the fact that supply was substandard. In that case of however; they have been only of some temporary shortage, which can be overcome.

7. The attempt should be to get food grains stocks, control as far as possible before the monsoon sets in. There should be adequate stocks in all the sub-divisional godowns.
8. Wherever dealers have stopped taking the supplies. They have to operated departmentally. In any case of continuous supply of food grains stock should be assured.
9. The system of getting works done through issue to be working in a satisfactory manner. There have been no complaints of any large scale malpractice but continuous vigilance should be there.[11]

Problems in Planning and Implementation

The average employment available in FFWP is about 30 days per beneficiary. Some wage employment beneficiaries have not got work for more than a week. Gram panchayat level works are normally small in nature generating term employment.

There is lack of people's involvement in identifying beneficiaries and works useful the village at the planning stage. The respondents also denied knowledge regarding formation of beneficiary committees after completion of works the two major complaints are they do not receive food grains in time or not receiving cash. The technical personnel have so many activities to do that they hardly have any time for their primary work helping in planning and monitoring. There were not uniform record keeping accounting practices and reporting. The village level officials do not have copies of the guidelines and have not been imparted with specific training that would help them in awareness creating beneficiary selection record keeping and implementation. These make monitoring and supervises cumbersome and inefficient procedure. Wage bill account for almost all of the total cost of the works in some cases giving rise to strong suspicion that material and equipment expenses have been clubbed in wage bill. Contractors have been involved in several works contrary to SGRY guidelines. This might be reflection of insufficient manpower, skill and other resources of implementing departments.

Problems faced by Implementing Officers as follows:

1. The technical staff was inadequate in the blocks.
2. There was shortage of account knowing staff in the blocks.
3. The output was very low as a large number of children and old women turning up.
4. A large number of posts of panchayat secretaries remain vacant.
5. The dealers were not lifting the stock due to unremunerative transport cost.
6. Technical staff was inadequate in various departments.
7. There are a number of remote areas where no fair price shops exists within a reasonable distance. Forest departments in particular experienced this problem as their works were situated in the interior.

After further discussions, the additional chief secretary indicated the following conclusions:

1. Moreover, works assistants are not available through being sanctioned to each block. It may take some time of them to join. However, they are best effort should be made with the available technical staff in regard to the various departments. The work under FFWP was relatively minor in comparison with their total workload and hence they should be able to do substantial work without additional technical staff.
2. The requirement of office staff for the block will be further examined and decisions will be taken at the government level.

3. Steps were being taken to fill up the posts panchayat secretaries.
4. In regard to the output additional chief secretary mentioned that the low output is due to a variety of reasons, such as women and children turning up. The workers were not working for the full period. Lack of proper supervision etc. all efforts should be made to supervise the works properly. It should also be insured that there is no question of bogus attendance—a false muster rolls. The question of flow output due to the employment of women and children will be further examined at govt., level. At the same time, the field officers may persuade the village pradhans from that family take the work.
5. As regards specifications for roads there was no provision under FFWP acquisition of land. Acquisition will also inevitably take a longtime. Hence, maximum possible efforts should be made to get land donated.
6. In regard to the taking over of roads after completion, the matter was already being examined at govt. level.
7. In regard to interior areas where there are no fair price shops near the place of work it has been decided to request the panchayat to open fair price shops. Certain procedural difficulties in this respect are also being resolved. Meanwhile DM will be pleased to make efforts to organize fair price shops in these places.
8. Some of the BDOs mentioned that the Director of Agriculture advised them during his tour not to engage, VLWs for FFWP. Chief Secretary mentioned that this was not the current position and the VLWs should be fully utilized Food for Work Programme, as this was the govt. policy.
9. The FFWP is one of the most important programmes taken by govt., for providing relief to the poorer section

in the village during the lean season. All officers should, therefore ensure that the works are taken up and implemented adequate funds and food grains have already been arranged and if there is any difficulty.

10. They may be brought to the notice of the DM who would get in touch with additional chief secretary. In any case there should be no case of starvation deaths in any village and for this purpose, a number of FFWP should be taken issued for utilization of funds under the panchayat sector for food.
11. Shortage of mechanics.
12. There are number of remote areas where there is no fair price shop within a reasonable distance.
13. Funds placed for maintenance of wells tube-wells is inadequate.
14. Roads constructed with PWD funds are not to the prescribed, standard of 12-0 width due to non-availability of land and other reasons.
15. Non-availability of cement road and pucca roads etc.
16. The involvement of panchayats as emphasis by the Chief Minister has to be ensured in all wards under FFWP. Actually this is due to the involvement of the panchayats and decentralized functions that it has been possible to employ a large number of workers in the villages under the programme.

The programme was intended to cater to the poor in villages and no poor man should be denied of employment and FFWP. This perspective should always be kept in view.

Selection for agencies for preparation of perspective plan must be done very carefully. Only reputed organizations/ institutions having expertise and competence to do such type of work should be considered and must possess adequate human resources with necessary skills to carryout field surveys, interact with local people and panchayat raj institute, conceive and design low cost projects. Use of local resources and draw up workable plans.

The selection of agency will be a committee chaired by the collector the other members can decided by the state government, which will prescribe parameters for short listing of agencies as well.

After the selection of the agency the collector will enter into a Mou with the agency specifying the details of work, time schedule and payment schedule. At least 25 per cent of the payment shall be made only the final approval of the perspective plan by the Ministry of rural development.[12]

Lapses in Implementation

It must be mentioned that it is not that administration cannot do much under these constraints in fact a lot can be done. Systematizing the implementation process of the FFWP can reduce intensity of constraints. However, our study shows that administration is not making sufficient efforts in this direction.

(1) Systematic efforts are not always made to assess the number of unemployed persons in the various villages at mandal level and to do the extension work to inform people about the FFWP consequently there are shortages of workers in the areas where people are poor and unemployed. Few works are taken up in the areas where workers are in plenty and infrastructural needs are urgent and large scale migrant workers are employed for FFWP works in rural areas which are relatively developed and which have a small number of persons belonging to the weaker sections.

(2) The way the FFWP is implemented the director of DRDA is able to effectively coordinate the implementation work at the district level. The horizontal and vertical linkages of functionaries of

the FFWP complicate the picture to such an extent that the result will not be satisfactory.

(3) The programme is not integrated with the programmes like the IRDP, MNP; FFWP district planning etc., FFWP treated more or less as an insolated programme and is implemented as such.

(4) A major objective of this FFWP is improve to the standards of nutritional level living of the poor. It is surprising that the implementation in most cases does not pay enough attention to the wage rates paid to workers or to the continuity of their employment, no statistics are collected about wages paid to FFWP workers. In some cases the officers were unable to tell us about the levels of the prevailing FFWP wage rates in their areas. When it was pointed out to them that some workers were getting low wages they said nothing could be done about that as so rates as fixed early.

(5) Constraints of staff and finance for example the 60:40 or 50:50 labour materials ratio have led implementers to use some ways. Which some times do not go well with the objectives of the limit employment of large scale migrant workers, use of labour cooperatives and gang leaders do not go well with the objectives of the FFWP. There is a need to formulate rules about these in the guidelines.

(6) One improvement of the FFWP over the earlier employment programmes is in the nature of assets. The FFWP lays emphasis on the construction of only durable assets and allots some funds exclusively for the assets, for the benefits of the SC/ST population our limited study of the assets however, has shown that not all of them are durable and what is classified as assets for direct benefit of the SC/ST population does not always benefit them.[13]

Problems Faced by Executing Agencies

Shortage of staff is the first major problem faced by the block agency in properly implementing the programme.

According to FFWP guidelines departments themselves have to employment the programme at the actual work level. That is panchayat samithi staff and village panchayats have to mobilize workers, assure their regular supply, procure required materials supervise the works, measure the work done periodically and pay wages and food grains to workers. Due to shortage of staff extension work of the FFWP is not done properly and data regarding the extent and nature of unemployment, people below the poverty line, small a marginal farmers are not collected and consequently planners do not know the availability of workers. It is necessary to provide more staff at panchayat level mainly at work site for implementing FFWP works, because sarpanch is the only person who practically looks after the construction works. A programme of the size and importance cannot be implemented satisfactorily with out adequate of staff.

It was observed that implementers found difficulty in maintaining 50:50 labour material ratio. It is difficult to spend to material component while on the other hand other implementations used various ways to reduce the material component FFWP in general mandays generated in a work is the progressive total of persons working on each day from its initiation to completion. The Zilla parishads while preparing the Annual action plan divide the wage component by the prevailing minimum wage rate for the calculating of man-days. Such a system is quite understandable and correct in the case of earth works as in these works there is no materiel component and their entire wages are paid to the unskilled labourers, in case of building works this is not true. It is necessary that the detailed guidelines how to maintain the labour cost material ratio should be provided to panchayat smithies to handle situation properly.

It was frequently complained that FFWP building works were not completed in some remote areas because sarpanch was not interested in going to remote areas. So it should be made compulsory for the sarpanch to complete the works within the given time.

In short, the problems faced by implementers are important in the sense that, if they are not solved. They are likely to have an adverse impact on rural areas. However, except for the shortage of staff all other major problems can be solved to great extent by systematic planning and by improving co-ordination between the block and panchayat administration.

The planning component was not satisfactory. FFWP guidelines are not sufficient to implement the programme. It is not just enough to give a list of objectives but also to lay down a priority rating in case some of them conflict with each other as they often do, allocation of funds is not done in systematic way and even not in time grant is released at the year ending, which hampers the completion of construction works in the given time.

Making the shelf of projects to know the felt needs of rural poor is a futile exercise because under the name of it some enlightenment areas are taken. DRDA does not implement the shelf seriously. The demands, from non-officials were always coming in the DRDA had to meet these demands the works were many times taken up on the basic of the suggestions of non-officials and ad-hoc considerations of the administration. FFWP is more or less an independent programme and has limited linkage with other programme like IRDP.

There is a lack of co-ordination among the various agencies involved in the planning for the FFWP. Neither the DRDA is able to bring level nor is the BDO is able to bring about co-ordination at the block level. There is a need of provide specific work wise guidelines for the proper implementation programme regarding the labour cost materials cost ratio under FFWP.

In some cases the individual's beneficiary spends and then receives more than payment in cash and kind in phases. This provision is meant to ensure that actual work. But it also means that such benefits can only be availed by those who can spend on their own to begin with. Alternatively providing assets to beneficiary after complete of work overburden government machinery lead the involvement of contractor and compromise on quality.[14]

Maintenance of Accounts and Audit

DRDA has been merged with district panchayat. The district panchayat shall be responsible for maintenance of accounts and Audit. The Account shall be maintained separately by each executing agency presented for audit.

In Effective Gram Sabhas in Identification of Work

The correct procedure for identifying community works was to hold a gram sabha meeting and then prepare proposals for works on the basis of that, the proposals would then have to be sent up to the gram panchayat for forwarding to the Mandal Parishad Development Officer. The Mandal Revenue Officer should also be involved at this level to approve proposals and ensure that no legal disputes would arise as a consequence of the works, and assistant engineer (AE) from the Panchayat Raj development would have to costing of the proposals in term of labour (and therefore rice) as well as cash requirements. Once these two procedures were completed, the proposals would be forwarded to the Collector by the MPDO. The Collector would be in charge of developing district wise proposals and estimate of the quantity of rice and materials that would be required. He would be responsible for the allocation of cash for different schemes. The primary objective was to create employment opportunities to the poor. The FFWP guidelines (both central and the state government) stated that labour intensive works were to be given preference. These included works under water conversion programmes (Neeru Meeru) watershed development works, water harvesting digging or desilting of ponds and tanks the construction of rural link roads and drains within the village.

However, practice was is different from theory. Gram sabhas which to identify FFWP were held only during first phase of the programme in our study villages, but even then democratic process was subverted in several ways.

The work that was actually approved reflected the priorities of the contractors who were invariably politically and socially powerful we discuss the issue of contractors in the following sections. In the second and longer phase of FFWP gram sabha were abandoned in favour of a more procedure in most cases local politicians. Engineers of other influential persons, some of whom were also contractors) proposed work, which were then approved by mandal officials and line department staff part of the reason for the pressure that government officials were being put under the complete woks in order to justify the large allocation of FFWP rice from the central government.

What is also striking from the key information interviews and focus group discussions is that most villagers in all locations did not know how much rice their village eventually received. Nor were they aware of their entitlement in terms of the amount of rice to be paid as wages and how they would get for work.

Both physical and financial audit of the works under the scheme are compulsory. This must be carried out at the end of the financial year by each district. The audit will be done either by local fund auditors or by the character accountants listed in the panel of the state government of wages of the state. The audit report together with action taken on the auditor's observations is required to be submitted along with the proposal for release of second installment of funds. Auditor should authenticate such action taken promptly.

Social Audit and Vigilance at Grass Root Level

- For every work sanctioned under this scheme, there will be a monitoring committee of the villages of the area to monitor the progress and quality.
- Every such committee shall have 5 to 9 members from the social workers, retired civil defense or private sector officials, other retired employees like teachers, well-educated persons, an SC, ST and women representatives.
- The monitoring committee will be constituted in the meeting of local beneficiaries convened by the local member of gram panchayat.
- The work cannot be started without constitution of monitoring committee.
- Monitoring committee would be appraised by the implemented agency about the estimate time frame and quality parameters of the works.
- The final report of the committee would be attach along with the completion certificate.

The awareness of FFWP programme wide publicity through audio, Video, Kalajatha press and wall writing is taken up in the selected districts.

A family card is to be issued to the identified labour in the each habitation for maintaining the records regarding supply of rice, cash and number of workdays.[15]

REFERENCES

1. R.K. Tiwari, Rural Employment Programmes in India, The Employment Process, National Rural Employment Programme and Evaluation Organization, Government of India, New Delhi March 1987, pp. 56.

2. Indira Gandhi, Labour Institute. Oxford (BH publishing Co. Pvt. Ltd. New Delhi, Bombay Calcutta, 1976, Ahmedabad, 1976, p. 60.
3. India Planning Commission, National Rural Employment Programme, Evaluation Organization, Government of India, New Delhi, March 1987, p. 25.
4. Wage Employment Programmes in Rural Development - A study of NREP in Gujart. Oxford IPSH Publication Co. Pvt. Ltd., New Delhi, pp. 81-83.
5. Deepa Bhatnagar, Food For Work Programme, A Study in context of Rajasthan pp. 287-301.
6. Wage Employment Programmes in Rural Development—A study of NREP in Gujart, n.4.
7. Food For Work Programme, Government of Tripura, Community Development Department, Compilation of orders, circulars and important decisions, pp. 83-63.
8. Guidelines, National Food For Work Programme, Government of India. Indian Institute of Public Administration, Indraprastha Estate, Ring Road, New Delhi-110002, pp. 11-15.
9. Food For Work Programme, Government of Tripura Community Development Department, n.6, pp. 83-63.
10. Guidelines, National Food For Work Programme, n.8.
11. *Ibid.*
12. Anitha Sharmas, Rural Employment Programmes in India, Mohit Publications, New Delhi 1994, pp.169-172.
13. Guidelines, Food For Work Programme, The Drought Affected Areas, Implementation Comprehension Government of Andhra Pradesh, Revenue Department Government Memo., No., 43951/ RIF.11/2001-3 Dated 20-9-2001, Adverse seasonal condition 2001-2002.
14. *Ibid.*
15. *Ibid.*

Operationalisation and Problems of Food for Work Programme

Eradication of poverty and providing employment have been one of the main goals of planning in India. The programme like SFDA, MFAL, DPAP, Antyodaya aimed at creating employment and livelihood opportunities to the weaker sections of the community in particular one of the recent rural oriented programmes is the FFWP which aims at integration of hunger and reducing the unemployment and creating of community assets in the rural areas.

The Ministry of Rural Development at the central level shall monitor the programmes through monthly quarterly and annual progress reports. The monitoring vigilance committees at the state and district levels the programme as per the guidance issued by the Ministry of rural development schedule for inspection of works.

For effective implementation of the programme, the state government will ensure that the officers at the state district, sub-divisional and block levels closely monitor all aspects of the programme areas, which desires the minimum number of field visits for each supervisory level functionary. It shall be drawn up by the state government and strictly adhered to the schedule. So drawn shall ensure FFWP works is atleast district level officer and in two panchayats by the state level officers a copy of the inspection schedule drawn. It will be sent by the state government to the Ministry of rural development for information, in addition the state government should advise the divisional commissioners collector and additional collector and sub-divisional officers of some works during their field tours.

The officers dealing with rural development FFWP at the state headquarters shall visit districts regularly and ascertain through field visit. The programme is being implemented satisfactorily. The execution of works is in accordance with the prescribed procedure and specification area officers for each district of the state and ensures. They undertake regular field visits to the area assigned to them.

During the course of inspection if any official comes across any unregulated he should immediately bring it to the notice of the project director who would then take appropriate action in the matter. A summary of the number of inspections conducted by district and state level officers shall be attached with the proposal for release of second installment of cash component of central assistance (reports and returns).

It shall be open to the central government to prescribe reporting format for monthly quarterly and annual reports. The state government may if it so desires call for such additional information in such formats as it may deem fit. The district panchayat DRDAs will also be accountable to the state government to ensure that the returns/reports in respect of the works taken up for execution under the FFWP in the districts are furnished in time [1].

Evaluation of Food for Work Programme

In 1979, the then Ministry of rural reconstruction felt that the FFWP instituted in 1977 should be evaluated so that the experience gained which assist in the formulation of suitable future polity. Accordingly the programme evaluation organization conducted a quick field survey of the programmes. Details of objectives of the study and its methodology are not spelt out here to avoid with repetition.

The Ministry of Rural Reconstruction is responsible for the general co-ordination and implementation of FFWP through the state governments. The programme was actually started in April 1977 and since the programme has been in operation for over. The ministry felt necessary to evaluate its working so that the experience gained may help in the formulation (or) modification of a suitable future policy. It was accordingly that the programme monitoring and evaluation organization of the planning commission should undertake evaluation study of the FFWP in the states in which utilization of food grains was considerable. Thus, the study was carried out in ten states, namely Andhra Pradesh, Maharashtra, Orissa, Haryana, Madhya Pradesh and Harayana, which had low utilization, were also included in the study, after presenting schedules and preparation of the design.

The arrangements for the distribution of food grains varied across states and districts. Distribution was mainly entrusted with fair price shops and village panchayat. Distribution was mostly carried out either through coupon-system or through muster rolls nearly 79 per cent of the selected beneficiaries were utilized with the system of distribution of food grains followed in their villages. Dissatisfaction was mainly due to the inadequacy of stocks, delayed payments remoteness of the distributing centers and over-growing in fair price shops. Some districts mystification prevailed despite checking.

The rate of utilization of food grains was generally low due to the late starting of the programme. The utilization of wheat and rice was 100 per cent in contain selected states.

The additional employment generated for selected household thoroughly by the FFWP. However, the beneficiaries revealed that the benefits were short-term and seasonal including some more items, which have relevance to the larger national objectives.[2]

Monitoring

All the rural employment programmes should be submitted of monthly and quarterly progress reports to enable proper planning and administration of the programme both at the center and the state levels. However "The inability to interpret satisfactorily under CSRE as between districts is partly the product of lack of property laid out monitoring system. The submission of monthly, quarterly and half-yearly progress reports were very much delayed known as to what is happening in that states. Physical achievement both in terms of the number of man days for which employment had been provided under various schemes as well as in the area brought under minor irrigation, soil conservation, aforestation and other schemes and roads constructed had to be reported fully and accurately. The information received was either incomplete or inaccurate it was difficult to analyze data and arrive at meaningful conclusion. It was observed in the FFWP, that monthly and quarterly reports were received with delay from months, one to six months respectively.

The review made in this has clearly shown that there has been considerable gap between the objective of the successive rural employment programmes and their outcome. At the same time, since the Sixth Plan, heavy reliance has been put on the overall framework of anti-poverty strategy on these programmes. This has resulted in providing more resources in these programmes. The implementation of the FFWP has been analyzed. The systematic examination of implementation will provide not only an examination of implementation of the constraints in achieving the objectives of this programme but also the basis to close the gap between expectations and effects so far as rural employment programmes are concerned.

The successful implementation of any programme is in effective monitoring and as often as possible. Therefore, implementation of the programme in the district collector would be monitored at the district level.

Such monitoring and review should be undertaken at least once in a fortnight. The district collector shall computerize the monitoring formats and make them available on line on a daily basis. The programme format in this regard will be furnished to the collectors by the planning department.[3]

Evaluation

Responsibility and accountability of implementation of the programme by the state government. It will be regularly monitored by the department of rural development, according with the existing in built mechanism through periodical reports vigilance and monitoring committee and visits by officers of the state government and by area officers of the Ministry of rural development. The programme will also be evaluated through reputed institutions/independents institutions/organizations as initiated by the centralized state governments.

Earth Works

In earth works we came across a number of problems, which are built under the panchayat sector, 'pucca' road construction. There is a provision of culverts proper alignment etc. Sometimes money is spent on the same work in subsequent, release of installment is also very pertinent to note that in a large amount approximately 25 per cent was spent annually under road construction in all the blocks. The road constructed is neither durable nor serve the purpose round the year. In a way the road works undertaken under the panchayat sector violate the norms as stipulated in the central guidelines. It is also important to emphasize that 15 to 20 per cent of grant under this programme was spent annually on earth works.

Another significant aspect both regarding works undertaken road and tank relate to the fact that in majority of the cases, the installment from the blocks was released by and large in month of May-June. This raises important questions both regarding the timeliness of the release of installments and commencement of such works in most of the cases was being observed that no attention was given to the timing of the works. It is common knowledge that the monsoon commences in both the districts by early June.[5]

Slack Season

It is also interesting to note that, even emphasis was not laid given completion of incomplete works of the same financial year, but a quite substantive number of works were opened under the panchayat sector.

Recovery

We came across many cases of recovery in the rural panchayats/block as well surveyed. The problem arises when either the sanctioned amount has not been utilised or less work has been executed in relation to the grant released to the sarpanches as valued by the sub-engineer. The delay in issue of the recovery orders is due to political interference.

Technical Supervision

It is expected from the sub-engineers of the RES to supervise the technical aspects of the work in panchayat sector. The valuation does not take place at appropriate time causing delay in release of installments and as a consequence of progress of work suffers. It was also commented by the sarpanch that they had to visit block office number of times to request the sub-engineer and the BDO to visit the work site for valuation and technical guidance some sarpanch complained sub-engineers demand money for valuation and if the money not given they try to under value the work. This problem as increased in all the areas. Even the sub-engineers and sarpanchs are not aware of the functions of this committee. The main reason being that the BDO's do not want to share the powers.

Durability

As visits of the sub-engineers are few at work site levels, it affects the quality of works. Though, it is difficult for us to comment on the cost estimates and specifications given for different building and earth works most of these estimated are based on current schedule rates.[6]

Maintenance

All buildings after their completion are handed over to the panchayat but they remain under the administrative control of the BDO's. Who hold responsibilities to maintain the building from their own funds. The panchayat are not willing to spend money on the repairs. There is no clear-cut policy regarding routine maintenance, leading to deterioration in the completed works, which can result in non-use of buildings after few years. It has been estimated that there is a need to make a provision of rural works for the annual maintenance.

Participation of the People

The gram panchayat involves both in the planning and execution of this programme. But this programme does not entail in public contribution in terms of cash or kind. There were certain isolated instances where the contribution of the people in terms of cash and labour the gram panchayat could construct more durable productive assets.

Utilization of Assets and Technical Design

The utilization of certain buildings like recreation hall and village secretariat complex constructed under the programme. In some gram panchayat instead of recreation hall, school building, and panchayat bhavan, there is a need to design and plan an integrated functional complex. This requires approach in the preparation of specifications and design on the part of the technical personnel.[7]

A number of sub-engineers pointed about defects in the specifications of the building works. It was pointed out in the design of school building. Three supporters were required which were not shown in the specifications.

Drawbacks

As noted earlier the programme has shortcomings both in its formulation and implementation. Dealing with formulatory aspect one finds that it is not clear from programme objectives. The programme is long-term strategy or only short-term relief measure concerned merely with distribution of foodstuffs. If it is presumed to be a short-term relief measure only, how are its objectives going to be achieved on the contrary if it is a long-term strategy about its success in future it solely depends on the food stock and present uncertain condition of food production government cannot risk depleting present buffer stocks.

Further, the programme reflects its limit operative capacity since operative sphere or working field of the programme presently includes only constructions and maintenance of rural assets. Government will have to saddle plan with more responsibilities making it broad based.[8]

Allotment of Funds and Valuation

Various aspects of the operational problems in panchayat, forest and PWD sectors, regarding the panchayat sector the works could be divided it parts – earth works and building works. Primarily in the case of building works their completion takes an average more than a year, it is also obvious from the table that in some blocks the installments were not released according to criteria laid down for their disbursement. In some cases, the grant was released in six to seven installments. The reason given by the BDO's were two-fold-firstly the installments were released according to the requirement of each case and secondly BDO's do not want to take risk in giving full installment, which might lead to their misutilisation fact remains that curtailment in the norms lead to delay in the completion of the works as such there is no continuity in the construction of the works. This also means that in building works different sets of labourers were engaged for different spells of time spread over a year or even more.

It was also noticed that the valuation of the building works as shown in measurements books various from one day to one week before released of the next installment. This is probably done it order to show that work lingered on the release of previous installment to the date of valuation and the release of the next installment, but in practice the problem of allotment of works valuation is normally conducted. Though, it is to establish whether the works were taken up immediately after the release of installment or not, all the same it is a confusing state of affairs. As pointed out earlier in building works if the grant is given within a reasonable period of time the sub-engineers and the BDO evaluate the progress of works regularly. It is possible to complete the works within a much shorter period than it is being taken up at the present. The present norms of release of installments and valuation should continue but it should be obligatory on sarpanchs to initiate the works within a week of the release of installment and there should be no break in the construction activity from the date of commencement to its completion. For this it is necessary to give this installment promptly. It is also evident that release of food grains did not synchronize with the release of cash installments. The quantity of food grains as assessed in the works was not provided and mostly cash was given to the labourers. Two progress reports were to be sent by collector, one of the state government and second one to the government of India.

Monthly Progress

This is to be submitted to the government of India by the district collectors.

Vigilance

The district collectors would frame a cell under their direct supervision to inspect the works at random and on receipt of complaints to ensure that the rice supplied under the programme is not missutilized.[9]

The District Panchayats/DRDA's will submit the following reports and returns to the states

1. A monthly progress report to be furnished in proforma by the 10th of every succeeding month as per it will be the responsibility of intermediate panchayat to submit consolidated report in respect of village panchayats and intermediate panchayat of that panchayat area by the 7th of every month.
2. A quarterly progress reports to be submitted by the gram panchayat and intermediate panchayat of that panchayat area by 7th of next month of the quarter ending.
3. A detailed annual progress report to be submitted by 25th April of the succeeding year. The Proforma to be used for this purpose is as per Annexure. The state government consolidates these reports and returns received from the district and furnish the same to the central government as follows:
   a. Monthly report by 25th of every succeeding month.
   b. Quarterly by 25th of every succeeding month and
   c. Annual report by 26th April of the succeeding year.

The reports would enable the authorities both at the state/ UT level to monitor the progress of the programme and to keep a close watch on the wage employment generated infrastructure. The central government may develop a computerized information system for reporting under the National food for work programme. All implementing agencies district panchayats/DRDAs shall follow the prescribed system.[10]

District Level Monitoring by Central Government

The Central Government will also appoint agencies for 100 per cent verification of works and test check of quality and cost. Apart from district level monitoring, national level monitors shall pay visit to inspect the works for which they will be assisted by the executing agencies.[11]

The ministry has taken up 27 states through locally based independent research institutions in130 districts. During the current year this mechanism enables the ministry to obtain not only the monthly physical and financial progress from differencing agencies but also generates periodic qualitative reports on the policy and implementation of environment programmes in the districts and verifications of physical achievements under different programmes. Such close monitoring helps in improving quality of implementation of progresses. The ministry has been regularly receiving monthly and quarterly reports agencies while the mcnthly reports give the latest financial and physical performance of the programmes.

The quarterly reports have been bringing out the issues, both positive and negative regarding. The implementation and policy environments in these perspectives district along with results of verifications of the physical progress. The information of success stories and good practices adopted by the implementing agencies are documented and reported.

The status reports on the points of national common minimum programme (NCMP) concerning the Ministry of rural development are as follows:

The UPA government will immediately enact a National Employment Guarantee Act. This will provide a legal guarantee atleast 100 days of employment every year to one able-bodied person in every lower middle class house in holds rural and urban areas.

The FFWP as approved by the cabinet on 13-10-2004 has been launched by the Hon'ble Prime Minister Rs.1951.66 crores and 20 lakhs M.T. of food grain has already been released to the identified 150 most backward districts. Cabinet has approved the draft National Rural Employment Guarantee Bill, 2004. The bill was already introduced in the lok sabha on 21-12-2004.

The UPA government will ensure that all funds given to states for implementation of poverty alleviation and rural development schemes by panchayats are neither delayed nor diverted monitoring will be under strict measure.

The Panchayat concerned will have the right to inspect and review the progress of any work under the scheme in its jurisdiction.[12]

1. State level discussion points.
2. District level discussion points.
3. Village observation schedule and
4. Beneficiary schedule.

The state level included aspects on administration and organization at state level food grains required. The state government faced difficult situation in obtaining food grains and achieved augment of the budgetary resources. The state government at the district level covered various aspects on administration and organization at district level release receipt and distribution of food grains agencies responsible and system followed for distribution of food grains. The information collected in the village observation schedule related to the agency responsible for implementation of procedure for taking up work in the village. The financial limit if any for the project rate of wage paid, its effect on the local wage rate of the programmes on local wheat/rice prices checks applied for misutilization of food grains durable community assets created. Their durability and extent of employment generated by the programme the amount of food grains requisitioned and received. The beneficiary income and employment of the beneficiary in availability of work in difficult years and its distance from the village or residence wage payment.

Monitoring for Efficient Implementation

The state governments/union territories shall make suitable arrangements for monitoring which is necessary for efficient implementation of the scheme. Apart from the district magistrate/collector, the steering committee in the districts, which shall be responsible for preparation of plans for taking up works under the programme and watching their progress, should ensure monitoring of the various works taken up in the districts. At the state level, the monitoring of works of various departments will have to be done by the heads of the implementing departments. There will have to be done by the heads of the implementing departments, which are members of the state steering committee. There should be supposing checks from the state as well from as the district level.

Monthly Reports and Returns

In order to enable the government to determine the quantum of stocks of what to be made available to state/union territory government under the scheme it is necessary that in the beginning of every year. The information regarding existing provision in the state/union territory government budget for on going and non-plan schemes new items of capital works as well as for maintenance of public works in respect of which food grains are proposed to be utilized should be furnished in the prescribed Proforma.

The progress reports will serve the needs of planning and administration of the scheme and it will enable authorities both at the centre and the state levels to keep a close watch on trends and apply corrective steps. The progress reports will form the basis for further release of food grains under the scheme. It is therefore, necessary that the state governments/union territories should furnish the monthly progress.[14]

Monitoring and Implementation

Implementation and monitoring are at district level and mostly in agriculture rural development and allied activities. The key to effective implementation of development programmes is local involvement. Through zilla parishads and panchayat samithis have been established in several states. The actual decentralization of political and administrative authority has been generally of limited system.

This gap came to be recognized in second five year plan itself which subsequently resulted in the establishment of three tier Panchyat Raj bodies at the village, block (taluka) and district level. On the recommendations of the famous Balwantrai Mehatha committees.[15]

Planning commission and chairman administrative committee appointed by the planning commission has given their detail reports as follows:

(a) Complete decentralization, administrative and financial at village and district level through three tiers Panchayat Raj institution.

(b) Political decentralization, involving people participation through their representative on behalf of Panchayat Raj bodies with real official machinery at all the three levels and

(c) All development programmes to be executed through official machinery alone.

Rural development officers should be members of this committee under the administrative control of the district development commission. The member secretary of this committee should be of the rank of a senior additional district magistrate, who should also be ex-officio chief planning cell for this purpose at the state head quarters and the planning evaluation organisation (P.E.O). The Planning Commission would carry out random sample surveys and publish them for general information, apart from forwarding them, the ministries and state governments with their recommendations fill up such gaps and weaknesses which may have come to their notice, this would ensure liaision with the zilla parishad. The Zilla Parishads should discuss the district plans at the formulation stage before the district development committee finally approves of them. The Zilla Parishads should also be authorized to review and monitor the progress of all the projects including in the district plans. These should be placed at the meeting of the districts development committees for suitable action. This should enable adequate participation of the local people at all stages of plan formulation implementation evaluation and monitoring. This would also largely avoid friction between officials and non-officials concerned with district plan.

We have adequate staff at the block and village levels to implement all the rural plans at the micro-level. At the state level, the commissioner and secretary agriculture production and rural development would be in overall control and supervision over the entire development machinery, both field and the secretarial level for monitoring. The state village monitoring committee with a view to revitalizing the role and functions of the vigilance monitoring committee for making them important instruments of effective monitoring of the implementation of the programmes of the ministry. These committees at state/Union Territories and district levels have been assigned a central role in the reconstituted elected representatives particularly the members of parliament have been assigned a central role in the reconstituted, the chairman of the reconsider vigilance and monitoring committee at district level. The other Member of Parliament is the chairman of the reconstituted vigilance and monitoring committee at district level. The other members of parliament representing the same district have been designated guidelines containing the composition, role and function of these reconstituted committees as well as instructions for conducting committees as well as instructions for conducting meeting have been issued to all the concerned, it has been stipulated that the meetings of these committees may be held on quarterly basis. These vigilance and monitoring committees replace all other committee's setup earlier for similar purpose. [16]

The major objective of the reconstitution and monitoring committees include providing a crucial role of the members of parliament and elected representatives of the people, in the state legislatures and to put in place a mechanism to monitor the execution of the schemes. In the most effective manner and within the given time frame as result of which the public funds are put to optional use and the programme benefit may flow to the rural poor the full measure. These committees would also keep a close watch over the implementation of the programme as per the guidelines meeting of the vigilance and monitoring.

The committees are effectively laising and co-ordinate with the Ministry of Rural Development and state governments to ensure that all schemes are implemented as per the programmes guidelines meetings of the vigilance and monitoring.

Committee at each level are to be held at least once every quarter after giving sufficient notice to all the members including honorable MP's/MLA's these committees constitute integral part of the system for the effective implementation of rural development programmes. There is no less significant than the audit reports and utilization certificates, which are mandatory for the release of second installment.

The Ministry of Rural Development has put in the place comprehensive system of monitoring for the implementation of the programmes including utilization of funds in order to ensure financial discipline. Audit reports and utilization certificates are insisted upon while processing the proposal for release of funds to the programme implementing agencies.

The carry out limit of funds from one year to another has been progressively reduced from 25 per cent, during 1998-99 to 20 per cent. During 1999-2000 it was further to 15 per cent, during 2000-01 graded cuts are also imposed on the second instalment if the proposals are received in December. The ministry has prescribed a procedure for timely release and utilization of funds in two installments. DRDA and Panchayat Raj institutions are actively involved in the implementation of the programme of the ministry, it is not feasible to release the funds directly to the agencies. [17]

REFERENCES

1. Guidelines, Food For Work Programme, Govt. of India, New Delhi, pp.1-15.
2. Public Accounts Committee 1981-82, Evaluation of Food For Work Programme, Rural Employment Programmes. August-October, 1979, p. 53.
3. Evaluation of Food For Work Programme, Programme Evaluation Organization, New Delhi, August – October 1979.
4. Planning Commission, Government of India, New Delhi, November 1980, pp. 4-5.
5. Guidelines, Food For Work Programme, Govt. of India, Ministry of Agriculture and Irrigation, Dept. of Rural Development Krishi Bhavan, New Delhi, 1978, pp.13-14.
6. S.C. Varma, Millions in Poverty Grip, Indian Rural Works Programme, pp. 96-97.
7. www.google.com
8. M.A. Quresh, Drought Strategy Plan Implementation and monitoring, pp. 60-65.
9. www.google.com
10. State Institute of Rural Development, Government of Kerala.
11. S.C. Varma, n.6.

12. Evaluation of Food for Work Programme, Rural Employment Programmes. August-October 1979, p. 53.
13. *Ibid.*, pp. 55.
14. Planning Commission, Government of India. New Delhi. November 1980, pp. 4-5.
15. Guidelines, Food For Work Programme, December, Govt. of India, Ministry of Agriculture and irrigation, Dept. of Rural Development Krishi Bhavan, New Delhi 1978, pp. 3-14.
16. M.A. Quresh, n.8, pp. 60-65.
17. Guidelines, Food For Work Programme Govt. of India, New Delhi, pp. 1-10.

Monitoring and Evaluation of Food for Work Programme

Main Findings

The conduct of the FFWP to the authorities concerned. No details of physical checking and inspection of works were available in two districts. No specific staff was sanctioned either at the center or in the states for the execution of the programme. The work was managed by utilizing the services of the existing staff through readjustment in nature and did not provide them a continuous and permanent income stream.

71 per cent of the beneficiaries reported that the workers under the FFWP were available within the village of their residence only less than 10 per cent received wages fully in cash. The rest in cash and kind or only in kind the wages paid in time only 52 per cent of the sample beneficiaries admitted. The wages paid under the FFWP sufficient to meet their daily expenses 45 per cent selected beneficiaries reported that the wages paid under the programmes were equal to the prevalent market rates; while 30 per cent reported that, the FFWP wages were higher than the market rates. Another 25 per cent maintained that the FFWP wages were lower than the markets rates.

Both plan and non-plan works undertaken incurred on creation of community assets. Construction of asserts like school building dispensary buildings, community halls. Some of the works could not be completed because of erratic supply of food grains and shortage of building material.

About 36 per cent of the selected beneficiaries admitted that their consumption levels had gone up due to the FFWP. The increase in course helped them in meeting above of their social obligations. Dearth and skilled hands made the local people learn non-traditional occupations like carpentry and masonary work. Despite these tangible developments it was apprehended and was evidenced income cases that the durable assets created under the programme of high benefit only the upper strata of the village community.

Major Suggestions

The question of expanding the scope of the programme to cover other activities, such as social forestry, plantation development, maintenance and beautification of ancient historical monuments in the rural areas may be considered since the majority of the rural people suffers malnutrition, it is suggested that the government may widen the range food grains distributed to include nutritional food items like milk, meat, cheese, fish and subhead.

Considering the opinion of the vast majority of the selected beneficiaries, payment of wages may be made on a daily or on a weekly basis, efforts should also be made to measure the works within three four days after their completion so that payments to the beneficiaries are made immediately thereafter. The arrangements for the distribution of food grains may be analyzed through the public distribution system in all the states on a uniform basis the Food Corporation of India should be directed to ensure the constant supply of food grains. The FCI may be made the sole supply and distributing agency unto fair prices shops. In order to locate the rural felt needs of the village's community it may be desirable to organize or activism local groups, unions associations and other voluntary agencies working for the welfare of the rural people.

The scope of the programme may be widened to include activities like constructions of houses for the weaker sections, construction of forest roads connecting remote villages, plantation of trees to withstand soil erosion development of handicrafts.

The study was undertaken in the Chittoor district of Andhra Pradesh a major recipient of food grains and which generated maximum employment under FFWP.

1. Among the studied households a high ratio of workers over 80 per cent belong to lower age group people engaged in the FFWP majority of these workers reported as wage earners in the previous year.
2. Almost all the beneficiaries belong to scheduled castes and scheduled tribe and backward classes and economically poor people. They have large families of high rate of illiteracy high. Dependent workers ratio, low income, and high rate of unemployment and under employment.
3. The incidence of poverty is observed to a great extent among the beneficiary householders, more than 90 per cent beneficiaries are below the poverty line defined in terms of per minimum desirable consumption expenditure. The selected households have limited value of assets but large financial liabilities, land and livestock accounted for a nominal amount for each of the household.
4. FFWP has generated extra employment to the workers under the study. An increase of 25 per cent in employment is recorded during the FFWP year over the previous one despite large number drought days. Additional employment undertaken by the beneficiaries in the FFWP has generated employment

opportunities income assets. FFWP has been contributing to about 45 per cent of the total work activities in the case of sampled households. This programme has replaced the wage labour as the main source of employment. Increased employment intensity per worker and more households in the upper strata of employment are also the other impact of the programme.

5. All the beneficiary households reported increase in their household's income since they started to work with the FFWP.
6. Additional income generated through FFWP has positively affected the level and better of expenditure of beneficiaries. There per capita and per household total as well as consumption for the beneficiary households smaller family size households is more dependent on their cereal requirements of FFWP supplies.
7. The caloric intake, calculated on the basis of adult units among studied households is higher than that of national average but far below than the recommended allowances by the nutrition advisory group (1968) for workers involved in heavy work.
8. There was significant impact on rural wages under the FFWP wages for all the agricultural operations and non-agricultural Jobs have gone up since the FFWP was introduced in the district. The impact was more at the beginning of the programme.
9. Remarkable fall in the prices of major food grains has recorded since the programme started in the district.

It is apparent form the foregoing analysis that the solutions for the most baffling problem of unemployment and underemployment, which have high concentration in rural area in India, can be found in labour intensive techniques.

But again such technology and product should not be pursued to the point. Wherein it may result in low productivity and creation of non-productive assets thus regarding the growth rate by wasting valuable scarce resources of the economy programmes like Antyodaya, FFWP, and minimum needs programme, which have been designed for giving jobs and reasonable living standards of the vulnerable rural sections of society. It is highly significant not only in helping the poor segments of society but in raising their meager purchasing power little on the one hand and creating national assets on the other such measures may have their impact felt in containing the price raise in the long run. Thus the FFWP as an instrument of job creation in rural areas has bright prospects if the programmes are well planned and coordinated and leakages are plugged.

The potential for FFWP to be self-targeting was defeated by wages being set above the market rate in less endowed villages. This drew slightly better off people away from out migration in the more productive and diversified locations FFWP wages were not high enough and few were willing to participate in the programme this high lights the need for better understanding of the labour market and agrarian relations among the policy makers both at the centre and the state. The case of FFWP reinforces recent thinking within the planning commission that mismanagement and misappropriation are more important causes of continuing poverty and deprivation. There are shortages of funds in themselves. Perhaps one way of avoiding such high levels of rice is released promptly so that cash payment does not have to be resorted. The pressure faced by District Collectors sanctioning works and distributing time also needs to be recognized. Further, transfers of this magnitude should not be allowed until such time as robust channels ensure that resources meant for the poor really can reach them.

On basis of the evidence gathered FFWP, some of the result has wider implications in respect of the effectiveness of the programme. At the existing wages, added employment has potentially raised the average income among the workers. The programme has not provided food for the people but also served social purpose through the construction of link roads and digging water storage ponds and tanks in the needed areas.

The programme has helped in migrating people from the hard hit areas of Chittoor District to the town and cities. The local people have started thinking that they will get food at a very reasonable rate if they work on a FFWP project but will starve if they go to towns and cities.

FFWP has helped in stabilizing the price of major food grains in the rural areas. Transfer of labour force from the local market to the FFWP projects has positively increased the wages in the villages.

It will take some time to see the change in infrastructure in Chittoor District, it requires more jobs. The urgent need is to plant the fast growing and steady grasses so that heavy rains do not wash away the earthwork grass planning can be taken for both the sides of link roads and embankments of ponds and tanks; it will be advisable to develop fish culture for further development of the rural areas.

There have been reports that block level officers, police, local leaders, FCI persons press reporters are involved in the other type of people wanted to take undue advantages of the situation which also had effected both the implementation of the programme in mandals. But, generally the programme is being implemented efficiently in most of the blocks in the districts.

The evidence shows how the very generous allocation of rice to AP, resulted largely due to the political leverage of the centre, did not translate into equally abundant employment for the very poor. The GOAP killed several birds with one stone by giving something to everyone—The poor, the local leaders and government officials. The benefits appears to have been heavily skewed away from the poor in this case compared to other employment generating programmes. Why the government used its leverage to obtain rice instead of cash, given the weak in the fiscal situation of the state. What appears to be plausible is that the government anticipated some linkages and also several direct and indirect benefits for the poor by flooding the market with rice but it does not expect misappropriation of such enormous quantities.

The potential of FFWP to be self-targeting was defeated by wages, which were theoretically below the market rate; the poor rarely command even the legal minimum wage. In most location FFWP did not attract very poor local labourers instead it attracted people away from out migration (and it is rarely the poorest who can migrate) as well as immigrant labourers. This highlights the need for better understanding of labour relations among policy makers both at the centre and the state.

Probably, the most disturbing message from this research work is that almost everywhere local leaders, politicians panchayat officials and particularly sarpanches have been heavily involved in corruption this calls into question the promise that decentralization holds for improved accountability and better service delivery. Although it could be argued that the motivations for this are generating cash because no real empowerment through fiscal decentralization has resulted in two doubts, (1) its cost effectiveness and (2) the dependency of the masses on the government.

In reply to the first objection we would like to stress that though cost consciousness is important the programme should not be evaluated strictly on the basis of the usual cost benefit analysis it should also be viewed in terms of its direct and indirect socio-economic lack of alternatives. Moreover if the programme is implemented properly their long-term economic and ecological benefits which could be very substantial and be amenable to measurement.

Finally, the programme proposed here is considerably different from the FFWP on rural Public Work programmes that have been implemented in India. So far the broad outlines have been formulated on the basis of experiences accumulated in many national and historical contexts and provide a sound basis for launching a concentration attack on the problem of poverty alleviation in India.

As a noted earlier the programme is productive and constructive coupled with the concept of human welfare but certain evils have crept in the programme both in its formulation and execution, therefore, their following suggestions are worth putting to improve the programme.

The mode of payment of wages partly in cash before making payment consent of the beneficiaries should be taken into consideration.

1. The government should burden the working sphere of the programme by including in its range some more programmes, which could provide technical skills to the beneficiaries. Thus rendering them capable of working in cottage industry or business in cycle works.
2. Gram panchayat should be directly held responsible for programme implementation.
3. Minimum standard should be prescribed PWS for maintenance and construction of works. These guidelines should be followed for the purpose of construction and maintenance under the programme.
4. Process of giving contracts to private contracts should be prescribed.
5. There should be different monitoring agencies at different level viz district, block and panchayat.
6. A FFWP cell should be constituted on lines of Antyodaya.
7. One set of surveying instruments is made available to each block.

8. To meet the paucity of technical personnel a short duration-training course in surveying and leveling is imparted to the select village level workers.
9. The district authorities should be empowered to take decisions suitable to local conditions as and when needed.
10. Only such roads sanctioned and undertaken which the village people are curious to have and are clear of encroachment.
11. Such pocket area should be identified where employment seekers are large in number.
12. Provision of constructing culverts and drains is made simultaneously. So that achieved work is protected from being crowded. It is observed that the village panchayats pay a certain percentage of commission for distribution to the agencies besides payment of handling and transport charges. It is suggested that should be made the property of the village panchayats from its sale back to the FCI. However, it will be appropriate for the ministry of rural reconstruction to issue uniform instructions to all the states. It is suggested employment opportunities should be increased income level higher wage rate and creation of community assets. The following are the suggestion measures in the light of the empirical study for effective implementation of FFWP:
    - Efforts should be made to provide food grains preferred by the beneficiaries.
    - Majority of the beneficiaries preferred weekly payments. As such, efforts should be made to make weekly and timely payments in all the areas.
    - It appears that he inspecting and monitoring arrangements at the centre for effectively supervising the FFWP and its implementation are rather unsatisfactory or far from satisfactory. Supervision, therefore, needs to be strengthened to avoid creation of non-durable assets.

— The Section banks should be increased.

— Cross bunds should be provided if feasible in large holdings.

— While creating the bund at a point where land belongs to two farmers, boundaries have to be clearly demarated. Through this may violate the principle of the contour, it will help in avoiding litigation.

— Cost benefit aspects of the assets should be created.

— Impact of the programme on the state and national economics including contribution to the state and national income.

The motivations for private gain and power cannot be used. Mechanisms for limiting corruption have not been effective. The case of FFWP also reinforces recent thinking within the planning commission that mismanagement and misappropriation are more important causes of containing poverty and deprivation rather than shortages of fund inflows.

The encouraging outcome is that the media is playing an increasingly important role as a watchdog and so is the multiparty system in the state, which provides at least some counter force to the government, phone complaints by the poor against people in positions of power may mark. The beginning of a new culture of voicing protest difficult challenges because simply formulating monitoring and checks and controls must be built in away that they cannot easily be falsified. At any rate the monopoly that the state and local elite hold in implementation needs to be eroded and they could be achieved by allowing in more independent agencies NGO's and the media into the process. But exactly how this can be done significantly would have to be worked out through further research and field trails. Until such time that resources meant for the poor are really reaching them further transfers of this magnitude should not be allowed.

Employment has been recognized as a socio-economic necessity. The process of economic development aims at giving employment to every person. However, further employment remains a myth in all societies. Hence, any attempt at socio-economic development should try to provide employment for the people in tune with their needs and abilities.

The discussion on the impact of the programme on employment of the beneficiaries reveals that the average additional employment under the programme comes to 57.94 mandays, which forms 2.39 per cent of their total employment or 40 per cent of their employment in the non-farm sector. The discussion on target group-wise generation of additional employment reveals that the landless labour depend more on the marginal farmers for additional employment. Similarly, the target group of scheduled castes depends, to a greater extent, on the programme for additional employment than the target group of Backward Castes and forward castes the discussion on scheme-wise generation of employment brings to light that the average additional employment created is more in the case of road laying activity than in construction activity which is attributed to the use of high cost material in the latter.

Thus, the foregoing analysis reveals that the target group of landless labour and labour from scheduled castes derive maximum advantage from FFWP in terms of earning additional income and deriving additional mandays of employment.

Operational Gaps in the Implementation of the Programme in the Study Area

The following defects are noticed in the implementation of the programme in the study area:

1. The works are being executed by private contractors in the name of village panchayats in contravention of the guidelines issued under FFWP.

2. The distribution of foodgrains is not satisfactory in some cases; rice is not at all distributed.
3. The workers engaged under FFWP are not completely aware of the provision that wage component consists cash and foodgrains.
4. The maintenance of NMRs is not satisfactory. Number of persons noted in the register does not tally with the number of persons who actually worked under the programme.
5. Daily reports of labour engaged on works are not sent to the concerned supervisory staff and the staff seems to be indifferent in this aspect.
6. Arrangements for the maintenance of assets created under the programme are not satisfactory.
7. The maintenance of records at the samithi level is altogether unsatisfactory. There is no timely submission of returns and reports with regard to the achievements under the programme.
8. There is no record at all of the assets created under the programme.
9. The utilization of funds is unduly higher in September and March leaving one out to suspect the correctness of such utilization on mass scale.
10. The technical and administrative wings do not have adequate staff for the effective implementation of the programme.

Though these defects impair the working of the programme, yet it is regarded as a food measure to provide security to the rural labour, which is proved by this field study. Thus the working of FFWP in the study area is satisfactory, despite lapses in implementation.

Other General Points of Significance

Labour cooperative societies or agricultural labour unions should be promoted and encouraged to take up works under the supervision of the engineering cell at the block mandal level. The contractors may try to force their way into FFWP. Perhaps the only way to check their infiltration into this programme is to have correct and tight fixed estimates and regular payments at prescribed rates for the prescribed work output. Then the contractors would have little incentive to intrude.

The practice of entrusting the task of transport and distribution of foodgrains to head mazdoor is not satisfactory. Provision should be made to give choice to the labourers in regard to the acceptance of foodgrains as a apart payment of wages. The Block Development Officer of the Deputy Executive Engineer should be allowed to purchase the necessary materials, if necessary, from the local market so as to complete the execution of work in time.

A number of field studies have identified that the officials have maintained bogus and inflated muster roles to cover up the deficiencies, in spite of the supervision of village level committees, the fact is, these committees are being dominated by nominated persons who are generally the supporters of officials. In order to avoid this problem, the village committees should give majority participation to the workers to enable them to know what is written in the muster rolls.

It should be recognized that more and more active involvement of people would result in speedy and sound execution of the works. To achieve this objective, all rural contribution must be encouraged at every step. It requires vast publicity of the various provisions of FFWP among the rural labour. They should know the estimates of the cost, duration of employment, date schedule of the works etc.

The allocations under FFWP are not enough to take up works in every village, if any meaningful percentage of the target group is to be benefited; the works have to be executed on a cluster basis. Mere spreading of resources over wide areas fails to rejuvenate the rural economy.

The present experience in the matter of maintenance of assets created is not satisfactory. Very often, the assets created are not taken over by the department concerned. The process of handing over the assets to the departments should be expedited and the procedure involved in this should be streamlined so that the interim period can be minimized.

To eradicate massive poverty and unemployment in rural areas, so as to create year round employment. But it should be remembered that FFWP is not the panacea for all the ills of rural poor. Employment generation is not synonymous with creating wage employment. It is necessary to combine the provisions of wage employment with the creation of conditions for additional self-employment. It is time switched over to employment oriented planning. Moreover employment oriented planning has a positive role in the present democratic context. These is pressure of growing population on limited resources. Unless creation of employment opportunities becomes the primary goal of planning and other objectives, the problem will continue to defy solution. It can be realized only in the framework of an expanding economy and dynamic well-planned agricultural sector.

Bibliography

PRIMARY SOURCES

Reports

1. **Evaluation of Food for Work Programme,** Evolution Organization of India, New Delhi, March 1987.
2. **Evaluation of Food For Work Programme,** Programme Evaluation Organization. August-October 1979.
3. **Food and Agriculture Organisation,** Report on the world food programme by the executive director, - Rome: FAG, 1 96$, VII, 99, p. 338.
4. **Food and Agriculture Organisation,** Women's leadership in rural development, Report on a National workshop to coordinate and plan for the women's group Programme, Institute of Adult Studies, august, 974, 'the FAO/UNFPA Workshop on population education in' Sri Lanka, 19-28 November, 1975, Rome, 1976, V. 48. p. 20.
5. **Food and Agriculture Organization**, Report on the FAO/ UNI-PA workshop on population education in the in service staff training programmes of rural development agencies in Asia and the Far East held in Peradeniya, Sri Lanka 19-28 November Rome, 1976, p. 48.
6. **Food for Work Programme,** A case study of Banda District, Agriculture Economics Research centres. University of Delhi-110007, 1980, p. 36.
7. **Food for Work Programme,** Agricultural situation in India, Govt. of India, Dept of Publications Civil Lines Delhi-110054.

8. **Food For Work, Government of Tripura,** Community Development Department compilation of orders, circulars and important decisions in meeting on Food For Work Programme issued/circulated by the Government of Tripper in community development Department pp. 83-63.

9. Government of Andhra Pradesh, Comprehensive Guide Lines **Sampoorna Grameena Rojgar Yojana** (special component). 27-01-2003. Government Memos. No. 71956/ RIF.II/ 2002 dated, 2-7-2003. pp. 9-10.

10. Government of India, Report of the Committee Unemployment 1973, p. 55.

11. **Guidelines, Food For work Programme, Government of Andhra Pradesh,** Revenue Department Government Memo. The Drought Affected Areas, Implementation Comprehension and NO. 43951/RIF.11/2001-3 Dated 20-9-2001 adverse seasonal condition 2001-2002.

12. **Guidelines, Food For Work Programme, Government of India,** Ministry of Agriculture and Irrigation Department of Rural Development, Krishi Bhavan, New Delhi, December 1978, pp. 8-9.

13. **Guidelines, Food For Work Programme, Revenue Department of Andhra Pradesh,** Government Memo.No: 43851/RIF11/2001-03, Dt: 20-09-20001.pp.8.

14. **Guidelines, Govt. of India, National Rural Employment Programme,** Ministry of Agriculture and Rural Development, New Delhi, August 1983, p. 3.

15. **India Planning Commission Quick evaluation study of Food For Work Programmes.** Programme Evaluation Organization, New Delhi 1979.

16. **India Planning Commission**, Evaluation of National Rural Employment Programme Evaluates Organization Government of India, New Delhi March 1987, p. 43.

17. **Planning Commission Government of India** Third Five-year Plan New 1962 chapter X, pp.154.

18. **Planning Commission,** Evaluation of Food For Work Programme, Final Report, Programme Evaluation Organization, Government of India, New Delhi,(August October 1-1979)

19. **Planning Commission,** Evaluation of Food for Work Programme. August -October (1979) Final report. Programme Evaluation Organization, Government of India New Delhi –110001 November 1980, pp. 10-13.

20. **Planning Commission,** Evaluation of Food For Work Programme: (August-October, 1979).331. 11 (54).

21. **Planning Commission**, Government of India Memorandum of Four Five-year Plan, New Delhi 1964, p. 24.

22. **Planning Commission**, Government of India approach paper to the Ninth Five Year plan (1997-2002) New Delhi: pp.16.

23. **Planning Commission,** Government of India First Five Year Plans New Delhi, 1952, p. 25.

24. **Planning Commission,** Government of India second Five-year Plan, New Delhi 1956, p. 109.

25. **Planning Commission,** Government of India Sixth Five-year Plan, New Delhi (1980-85), p. 210.

26. **Planning Commission,** Government of India, Approach Paper to the Ninth Five-year Plan New Delhi, (1997-2002), p. 13.

27. **Public Accounts Committee** 1981-82, Evaluation of Food For Work Programme, Rural Employment Programmes. August-October 1979, p. 53.

SECONDARY SOURCES

Books

1. **Anita Sharma**, Rural Employment Programmes in India, Mohit publications New Delhi.

2. **Barret, C.B. Holden, S Clay**, Can Food For Work Progamme reduce vulnerability, Department of Economics and Resource Management Agriculture University of Norway, 2003.

3. **Bhandari S.S** "New Scheme launched in Eighth plan, Allocation stepped up for Rural Development" Grameen Vikas newsletter (Vol, 13, No. 2, February 1997) pp.8.

4. **Deepak Bhatnagar**, Rural Development in India. Economic Programme, p. 45. Delhi, pp.1-15.

5. **Depa Batnagar**, Food for Work Programme, a study in context of Rajas tan, pp. 287-301.

6. **Desai Vasantha**, Rural Development issues problems Vol-1 Bombay Himalayan Publishing House 1988, p. 2.

7. **Edward.j. Clay**, Rural Public Works and Food For Work. A survey, institute of Development studies, University of Sussex, Brighton, UK.

8. **Hanumanthan**. **C.M.** Evaluation of Food For Work Programmes in Soil Conservation work/by: Planning Department, Bangalore, 1982, V.58, p. 20.

9. **Kanna.. B.S.** Rural Development South Asia, Policies and Programmes, pp. 157-158.

10. **Lakshmaih,** K National Rural Employment Programme, A Case Study of Chittoor District, M.Phil Dissertation, Department of Economics, S.V. University, Tirupati.

11. **Priya Deshingkar, Craig Johnson**, State Transfer To The Poor and Back, The Case of the Food for Work Programme in Andhra Pradesh, Overseas Development London, SEI Development Institute U.K. October 2002, pp. 25-40.

12. **Rao**, **GVK,** Food For Work Programme, Secretary, Ministry of Agriculture and Irrigation Govt. of India Kishi Bhavan, New Delhi August 1978.

13. **Rebello N.S.P, Hanumanthaiah. C.M.**, An Evaluation of Food For Work Programme, Soil Conversation Work, Evaluation Division, Planning Department, Karnataka Government Secretariat, Banglore 1982, p. 30.

14. **Sharma**. **R.D.** Guidelines, Food For Work Programme a case study of Banda district A.G. Economics Research center university of Delhi-110007, 1980.

15. **Sing**. **N.P.** Food For Work Programme, Ministry of Rural Reconstruction, Government of India, Agriculture situation in India, April 1980, p. 82.

16. **Tiwari, R.K, Rural** Employment programmes in India, The Employment Process. India Planning Commission on Nation Rural Employment Programme, Evaluation Organization, Government of India. New Delhi, March 1987, p. 56.

17. **Varma S.C,** Millions in Poverty Grip, Indian Rural Works Programme, pp. 96-97.

Journals

1. **Asaduzzaman,** M. and Huddleston, Barbara an "Evaluation of management of Food For Work Programme", Bangladesh Development Studies, 11 (1 & 2), 1983 (March-June), pp. 41-96.
2. **Ashok Mitra**, "Nutrition Food for Work and Stumbling Block", Main Srearm p. 29.
3. **Ashok Mitra**, "Food for Work should aim at Nutrition", Kurukshetra, July 16, 1980, pp. 14-17.
4. **Basu, Kaushik,** "Food for Work Programmes", "beyond roads that get washed away", Economic and political weekly, 14 (1 & 2), 1981(January 3-10), pp. 37-40.
5. **Chowdhurty**, "Food for Work Programme in Bangladesh". Bangladesh Development Studies, 11 (1 & 2),1983 (March June), pp. 111-134.
6. **Clay, E.J**, "Rural Public Works and Food For Work; A Survey", World Development, 14(10/11), 1986 (Oct-Nov.) pp. 1237-1252.
7. **Dandekar, Kumudini and Sathe**, Manju "Employment Guarantee Scheme and Food for Work Programme". Economic and Political Weekly, 15 (15), 1980 (April 12) pp.707-713.
8. **Dandekar, Kumudini and Sathe**, Manju Impact of "Food for Work Programme" Kurukshetra, 28 (17), 1980 (June 1), pp. 8-15,
9. **Food For Work Programme**, "Final Evaluation", Yojana, 26(9), 1982 (May) 29, pp. 16-31.
10. **Food For Work Programme**, A Case Study of Banda District, Agricultural Situation in India, 36(3), 1981 (June), pp.181-182.

11. Food for Work, *Eastern Economist*, 73 (3) (9), 1979 July - 20).

12. **Ganesh Kumar, Srijit Mishra, Manoj Pande**, "Employment" Guarantee for Rural India, Economic Center, 18, 2004, p. 10.

13. **Gupta, D.P.** "how goes The Food For Work Programme – A Case Study", Kurukshetra, 26 (23), 1978 (September 1): pp.16-17.

14. **Gupta** "How goes to the Food For Work Programme a case Study", Kurushetra September 1, 1978 pp.16.

15. **Kalipadu Basu**, "New Economic Policy for Generation of jobs Opportunities", *Yojana* vol, xxiii, March 16, 1979, p. 18.

16. **Kaushik Basu**, "Food For Work Programme" Economic Political Weekly, January 8-10-1981. pp. 37-40.

17. **Kumudini Dandekar, Manju Sathu**, "Impact of Food For Work Progamme", and Kurukshetra June 1980, pp. 8-14.

18. **Lionel Messias**, "Right of Food", Human Scope India, vol. No. 1 Issue February 11, 2003.

19. **Maxwell, S.et.al,** "The Disincentive Effect of Food for Work on labour supply and agricultural intensification and diversification in Ethiopia". Journal of agricultural Economics, 45 (3), 1994 (September): pp. 351-359.

20. **Mitra, Ashok,** "Food For Work, Should Aid at Nutrition" Kurukshetra, 28(20),1980 (July 16) pp. 14-17.

21. **Mitra, Ashok,** Food Nutrition, "Food For Work and stumbling blocks" Mainstream, 18 (34), 1980 (April 19), pp. 31-33.

22. **Mitra**, S.K. "Food For Work Programme an employment booster". Yojana, 23 (1 & 2), 1979 (January 26) pp. 17-18 & 53.

23. "National Food For Work programme corrupt". Down to earth, 14(5), and 2005 (July): pp. 22-33.

24. **Osmani, S.R. and Chowdhury, O.H** "Impact of Food For Work Programme in Bangladesh". Bangladesh Development Studies, 11 (1 & 2), 1983 (March-June), pp. 135-190.

25. **Panda, Manoj Kumar,** "Productivity Aspect of wages in Food For Work Programme", Economic and Political Weekly, 16 (20), 1981 (May 16), pp. 922-923.

26. **Pant, S.P.** "Poverty, unemployment and Food For Work", Agricultural Situation in India, 35 (2), 1980 (May) pp.83-90.

27. Prasad Rao DVLN, "operational dynamic of NREP in Kerala", Kurukshetra, Vol. No. XXXIII 12 September 1985.pp.28-30

28. **Rao, G.V.K.** "Food For Work Programme", Intensive Agriculture, 16(6), 1978 (August). pp. 5-7.

29. **Rudder datt,,** "Employment Guarantee Act", Janatha, February 6, 2005, p. 9.

30. Rural employment programmes. August-October 1979. p. 53.

31. **Shibli, M. Abdhllah,** "Food For Work Programme": "beyond roads that get washed away- a comment". Economic and political weekly, 16 (22), 1981 (May-30), pp. 994-996.

32. **Shrimathi Indira Gandhi**, "Food For Work Porgamme", Final evaluation, Yojana, 16-31 May 1982, pp. 40.

33. Simla, Ministry of Labour, Labour Bureau, Indian Labour Book 1985, pp. 23.

34. **Sing NP,** "NREP" "problems and prospects of Rural youth", Kurukshetra, volume No. XXXIII, 5 February 1985, pp. 10-13.

35. **Singh N.P,** "Food For Work Programme makes headway", Agricultural situation in India, 35 (1), 1980 (April), pp. 3-13.

36. **Singh, Prabhu Nath,** "dimensions of rural unemployment and Food For Work Programme". Southern Economist, 18 (21), 1980 (March), pp. 20-25.

37. **Singh, Prabhu Nath,** "dimensions of Rural Unemployment and Food For Work Programme". Khadi Gramodyyog, 26 (1), 1979 (October).

38. **Singh, Prabhu Nath,** "Rural Unemployment and Food for Work Programme". Khadi Gramodyyog, 26 (1), 1979 (October).

39. **Sings V.S.** "Poverty Alleviation Programmes in operation: An Assessment" Kurukshetra (Vol. XXXVI, No. 7, April 1988).

40. **Smt. Indira Gandhi**, "Garibi Hatao. Can IRDP Do it? Discussion" Economic and Political Weekly (Vol. XX, No. 13 March 30 1985)

41. Socio-culture Indian, India starts Food for Work Programme, Southern Economist, June 15, 2004, p. 3.

42. **Sri Mishra, Sangita, Mallikarjuna Tondare,** Evaluation of Food for Work, Component Sampoorna Grameena Rozgar Yojana (SGRY) in selected districts Report submitted to Planning Commission of India.

43. **Srinivas,** M.N. "Reflection on Rural Development", Main stream Vol. XVII, No. 47,12, May 1979.

44. **Subrata Benerjee,** "I.I.O. Comment of action against Un-Employment Planning for full Employment", Yojana vol, XXIII, January 6, 1979, pp. 57-59.

45. **Swami Das Gupta,** "Institutionalizing Corruption through Rural Job Scheme", Future Samachar, pp. 1-4.

46. **Thukral, R** "how goes the Food For Work Programme", Kurukhetra, Vol. XXVIII, No. 12, March 16, 1980, pp. 4-14.

47. **Tilve, Shobha and Pitre**, "Vidya Employment guarantee shake and Food For Work Programme", a comment Economic and Political Weekly, 15 (47), 1980 (November 22) 1988-1989.

48. **Tiwari R.K.** "Rural Employment programme in India; The implementation process", Indian Institute of Public Administration, New Delhi, 1996, pp. 96.

49. **Varma, S.C**, "Providing work to the Rural Poor", Kurukshetra, 30 (6), 1981 (December 16-3), pp. 4-5.

50. **Varma, S.C,** Millions in Poverty Grip "India Rural Works Programme", Kunj Publishing House, 16, Panchaseela Enclave market, New Delhi- 110001, pp. 96-120.

51. **Ved Basin**, "Massive work under Food For Work Programme", **Janata,** and July 1979, p. 5.

52. **Venugopal Rao, M** "Large Scale Misuse, Under Food For Work Programme", Communist Party of India, People Democracy, Vol. XXXVI.

53. "Who cares for Rural Poor", Commerce, 141 (3619), 1980 (November 1) pp. 828-829.

News Papers

1. Andhra Jyothi (Telugu Daily)
2. Business Front Line
3. Deccan Chronicle
4. Eenadu (Telugu Daily)
5. Frontline
6. India Today
7. Indian Express
8. The Hindu
9. The Week

Websites

1. www.google.com
2. www.ap.nic.in
3. www.ap.ruralnic.in

Index

R

S